MORE THAN A MUM

Rediscover the woman within for a happier, balanced life

NIKKI COX

NIKKI COX

Copyright © 2019 Nikki Cox

All rights reserved. No part of this publication may be reproduced, distributed or transmitted in any form or by any means, electronic or mechanical, including photocopying and recording, or by any information storage and retrieval system, without the prior written permission of the publisher, except where permitted by law.

Published by Nikki Cox Consulting
nikki@nikkicox.com.au
www.nikkicox.com.au

First Edition
Book and Cover design: Nikki Cox
Editor: Jami Leigh Acworth

ISBN:
978-0-6485124-0-0 (Print)
978-0-6485124-1-7 (E-Book)

Testimonials

It's good just to stop and think about things… life gets busy and just takes over. Thinking about priorities, goals and what means the most to you is important. Thank you, Nikki.

Danielle W.
Working mother of two

I love what you are doing for mothers like me. You are inspirational and have such a powerful and positive impact on many of us women, who need this in our lives.

Rebecca O.
Working mother of one (with one in the oven)

I found 'More Than A Mum' to be thought-provoking… it ends up being so valuable to you *and* your family!

Terese T.
Stay-at-home mother of one

Nikki gave me an opportunity to look at myself and my life in a way I never have before. I was able to identify my inner strengths and passions, and apply them to many different areas of my life.

Irene D.
Carer and job-seeker

I was able to narrow down what my current goals are and what I really want to achieve, so that I could be and feel like more than just a mum.

Miram M.
Homeschooling mum of three

I really liked working with Nikki... just what I needed at the time. Thank you.

Jessica S.
Small business owner and mother of one

Nikki helped me brainstorm what would and wouldn't work to achieve my goals in life, without me feeling judged or overwhelmed.

Autumn T.
Student and entrepreneur

Contents

Introduction	1
Who Are You, Mum?	5
Unload the Mental Load	25
Mindfulness Matters	41
Refill Your Cup	55
It's Time for You	69
Take Control of Your Happiness	83
Strengthen Your Bonds	101
Love What You Do	117
Energy Synergy	135
Bedtime Blessings	151
Nurture Your Senses	165
Eat With Your Mind	179
Afterword	197
About The Author	200
Work With Nikki	202

NIKKI COX

Introduction

When you become a mother, something fundamental shifts inside of you. Every fibre of your being is devoted to learning how to parent, and how to do it to the best of your ability with each challenge that comes along. You give up large parts of yourself to nurture and care for your children; mentally, emotionally, physically and socially. And whilst these are willing sacrifices, they don't necessarily slow down as your kids grow.

So many mothers today are experiencing loneliness, depression, anxiety, burnout and isolation due to lack of support and resources. I was one of them. This is because the reality of parenting today has changed dramatically from when we were brought up. More and more women are moving away from their networks of family and friends for careers, partners or a better lifestyle for their children. But the old adage 'It takes a village to raise a child' holds enormous truth; we can't go through motherhood alone.

Throughout this book, I will share with you my own struggles with becoming a mum to two beautiful children whilst juggling a career and living with Fibromyalgia. I will also provide you with stories of other mums that have faced struggles similar to yours on their journeys through motherhood.

But there's not just stories inside; this book will also share with you the tips, tools, strategies and habits I have created and used in my own life to become more than just the role of 'mum'. During my own struggles, I was determined to find a better way of living as a woman with kids, so I returned to university to study positive psychology and wellness. The strategies I offer you in this book have been developed either from my own experiences, or have been adapted from my studies to be easily integrated into a busy mum's lifestyle.

It is my deepest wish to help mums cope with the challenges that come with being a woman with kids in today's world, well beyond the first few years of motherhood. Being a mum is a tough gig; it's a role that is relentless yet undervalued, unappreciated and often dismissed. I believe mums are amazing, and deserve to live a life of happiness and equilibrium. More than this, I believe all mums deserve to feel like a Supermum. So embrace the super powers that this book has on offer, and so much more.

This book will help you to recreate your village and the support it provides; and it starts with reconnecting you with the woman that exists inside you, outside of "mum... Mum?... MUM!!!!" To understand who you truly are allows you to live a life that balances your wants and needs with those of your kids. It builds the resilience and strength you need to handle the challenges of motherhood, well beyond the toddler years. It creates a happier version of yourself, which creates a happier family life.

Many mothers I have worked with have committed to using the strategies from this book in their own lives because they create *real* change. Like me, they are living happier, more passionate lives that are full of energy, optimism and balance. Like me, they are able to control their guilt and stress through improved self-awareness, connections with others and time management.

I promise that, if you commit to implementing the tools and strategies provided in this book, you can live your life as more than a mum too. I promise that you can regain control over your stress and energy levels, the quality of your sleep, your negative thought patterns and your feelings of loneliness and isolation. I promise that you can love work again and be more resilient in the face of life's challenges. I promise that you can feel less guilty and more confident with the decisions you make in life. And the sooner you start, the quicker this can become your reality!

I encourage you to begin this book with a pencil and a journal, or notebook, handy. Then, taking one chapter at a time, watch as you make small discoveries along the way to find the best strategies for you to make positive changes in your life.

1

Who Are You, Mum?

Does your life currently revolve completely around your kids? Have you found that you have stopped caring about how you look? Are you so busy being a mum that you actually feel lonely or isolated? Do you feel like your identity is completely tied to the career you had before you had kids? Are you regularly missing the freedom you once had as a woman without children?

If you answered yes to one or more of these questions, you may be travelling through motherhood whilst in the middle of an identity crisis. Identity challenges often appear during times of change, and life certainly does change when you become a mum!

"I don't know who I am anymore" is often heard and felt by many women who are struggling to adjust to life with children. Becoming a mother can feel like living in a paradox of grieving the loss of who you once were, while clearly knowing that you wouldn't trade your life with your kids for anything.

When I first became a mother, I honestly struggled. My sense of self-worth was tied directly to my skills and talents at work, which became somewhat useless in the role of a mum. Even after I returned to work, I couldn't find the passion and drive I once had for the job before I had my daughter. Something felt 'off'; something was missing. I kept feeling the overwhelming guilt for wanting to be me again instead of just being a mum. Not a day went past where something wouldn't trigger me to tears; eating lunch on my own; the commute home taking longer than normal; an overly constructive performance review meeting of my team; a beautiful, sunny day that could be spent at the park.

The return to the working world is only one way your identity may be challenged once you become a mother. You may be one of many women who believed that becoming a mother would define who you are, that raising children is your purpose in life and you expected that having children would be completely life fulfilling. Whilst I have no doubt you still feel this way, it can still be quite a shock to feel the sense of identity loss as your life revolves almost entirely around your kids, bringing with it feelings of loneliness and isolation.

The scariest part of going through an identity crisis is not knowing what your future will look like. Asking yourself questions like "How long am I going to feel like this?", "Am I going to feel less like my old self years down the track?" or "If I ever find myself again, will I even like who I am?"

No one can control this transformation to 'mother', but rather than being unconsciously carried down the river of change, you can learn how to participate in this transition more consciously, through identity awareness and acceptance.

♥ ♥ ♥

Motherhood often brings with it a sense of identity loss. Dr. Alexandra Sacks, a widely recognised clinical expert on the developmental transition into motherhood, says that 'giving birth to a new identity can be as demanding as giving birth to a baby'. How true!

Becoming a parent is a HUGE transition and you probably haven't taken the time to fully adjust to the change. Don't worry, very few mothers do. It doesn't matter how prepared we think we are, becoming a mother can still be overwhelming, scary and strange. The trouble is, we then get stuck identifying with a past version of ourselves and what life used to be like.

But this is the only reason why you feel like you've lost your identity; you are still trying to identify with a you that *doesn't exist anymore.*

A little while after becoming a mum, I would think about the times I spent with friends just chatting (or dancing!) the night away. I would criticise myself for being 'boring' and 'less exciting' than who I was before. I'd long for the joy and independence I felt travelling interstate for work. All of these thoughts would then be immediately followed by guilt. Guilt for even thinking such things. I'm a mother of a beautiful little girl; how *dare* I think about being anything other than her mum and her world!

Your brain loves to identify with the past. Past life experiences have taught you to attach your identity to a picture of how life is supposed to look, in order for your life to be valuable. Feeling lost is just your mind's way of saying it has lost its ability to play out roles you have come to believe define your worth.

It was this realisation that set me on my own path of self-reflection and personal insight. I was *done* feeling guilty and critical of my own thoughts, feelings, and choices. I was *done* feeling lost, empty and isolated in my so-far short experience of being a mother. My academic training in psychology was screaming at me, by this stage, that there was a better way, that life (and motherhood) was not meant to be experienced this way, and that there was a solution to be found.

I needed to find out what I wanted from life, now that my daughter was in the picture. I had to find what brought me joy and excitement, and I had to realise that things were different from how the 'pre-mum' me received personal nourishment and fulfillment. I just wanted to feel like *me* again; comfortable in my own skin and confident to make changes and decisions for my life.

When you become a parent, you need to learn to accept that who you once were has changed. Your identity isn't lost, it's just buried under nappies and school books. But you can slowly start to find yourself again.

Dr. Sacks describes the process towards identity awareness and acceptance as a mother as:

> *'a dance, where you lean in to take care of your kids, but you have to lean out to take care of yourself. Because you're still a human being, and you still have to care for your own body, your own emotions, your relationship with your partner, with your friends, your intellectual life, your spiritual life, your hobbies [...] all these other aspects of your identity and your basic needs. Even if you want to just give*

unconditionally to your children, you can't, because we're humans, we're not robots.'

What if I don't like who I am now, compared to the person I knew before I had kids?

After having kids, you grow a lot as a person. You've just never had the chance to sit down and meet the new you! I, personally, found that I was trying harder to do better at things in life, such as eating healthier, getting outside more, being kinder and more grateful. I had become better at letting go of the little things and was *far* more organised.

If you are typically the kind of person that doesn't like to meet new people, it usually means you are afraid you won't be liked, accepted or 'fit in'. Meeting the new version of you won't be as scary, trust me. You will still see parts of you that haven't changed, and if you discover some of the new parts aren't to your liking, there is no reason why you can't take steps to change!

You *could* go on living your life for years not knowing who you really are and what you really want from life. This feeling can last for many years, well beyond when your kids were first born. But wouldn't you rather live a life full of passion, purpose, and happiness? A life more than just being a mother to your kids?

My identity journey took over 10 years' experience in adult learning and development, an undergraduate degree in

Psychology, a career change, the birth of a second child and a post-graduate degree in Wellness to find… but yours doesn't have to. In this chapter, I will guide you through practical ways to find *your* new identity, and your passions, as both a mother and a woman.

♥ ♥ ♥

When people used to ask the 'pre-mum' me who I was, I would clearly and confidently say "I am a learning and development professional that loves to teach people face to face, but also specialises in elearning development because I am a nerd and a gamer at heart". I knew who I was, what I wanted and what I enjoyed in life.

After I became a mum, my answer was somewhat less definitive, and always began with "I am a mum…" Was I still considered a professional if my mind and heart now felt 'split' between being a mother and being an employee? Am I still a nerd and a gamer at heart if I no longer have time for those things?

We often find our identity in *what we do* as opposed to *who we are*. This is why we try to identify ourselves solely as our job role or our daily activities. It's also why so many women struggle to see themselves as more than a mum.

When you ask someone who they are, you'll often get responses like "I am a nurse / a teacher / a childcare worker / a volunteer / a homemaker". But people are more than what they do for a living; it does not define us as human beings.

I want you to reflect on the following key questions:

- What do you want right now?
- Who do you want to be?
- How do you want to feel?
- What experiences would you like to have?

You may not know how to answer some (or all) of these questions right now, but the goal of this book is to get some solid strategies along the way of how you would answer them. Someone who is clear on who they are and their core identity can answer these questions without hesitation. And this sort of clarity on your life is fundamental to making good decisions and positive changes.

To start finding who you are, we first need to breakdown the parts that make up your own identity.

A 'pivot' is the central, most important point in a situation that supports something that turns or revolves. As a mum, I believe you are the pivot of your family; the person they fundamentally depend on.

Your identity is *your* pivot:

- P   personality
- I   interests and hobbies
- V   values and beliefs
- O   occupation, and
- T   talents and skills

Before I go into each of these parts of your identity, it is a good idea to start mapping your identity journey out. Writing things down is not only helpful for remembering, but it can also be useful for reflection and seeing the connections between different concepts and dimensions.

Grab a notebook or journal, and on the first page draw five circles, labeling each circle a different part of your identity (see below).

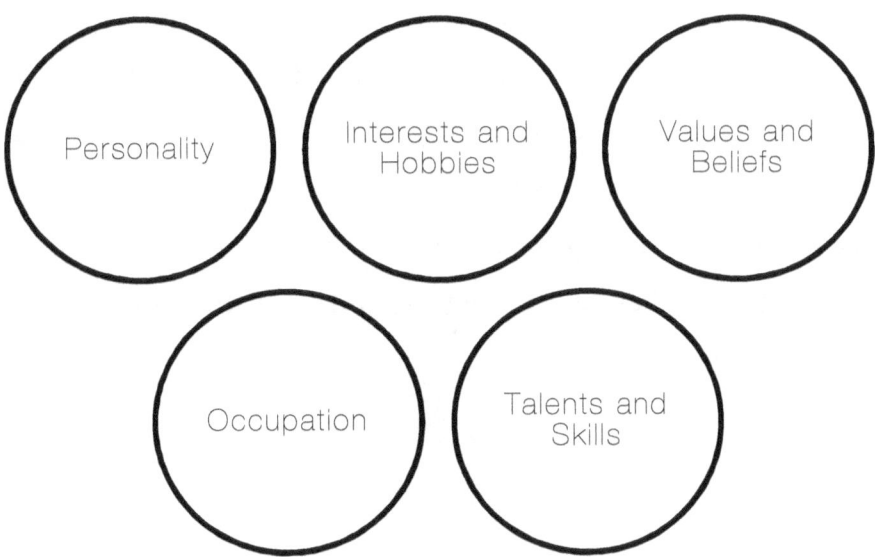

As you read through the rest of the chapter, draw arrows from each of the relevant circles to key words or phrases that represent and reflect who you truly are, to complete your personal identity map.

Personality

Our character strengths are the defining parts of our personalities that form our identity. By clearly identifying what your core, personal character strengths are, you can use them to redefine who you are, what you want from life, and how to get where you want to be.

The VIA Institute has developed the world's most recognised, psychometrically validated survey to help people identify their personal character strengths. The full survey is approximately 200 questions long, but I strongly encourage you to complete it and get a personalised report outlining your 24 character strengths, in order (available at www.viacharacter.org/www/The-Survey). Once you know your top five character strengths, add them to your identity map.

This is what my identity map looks like at this point:

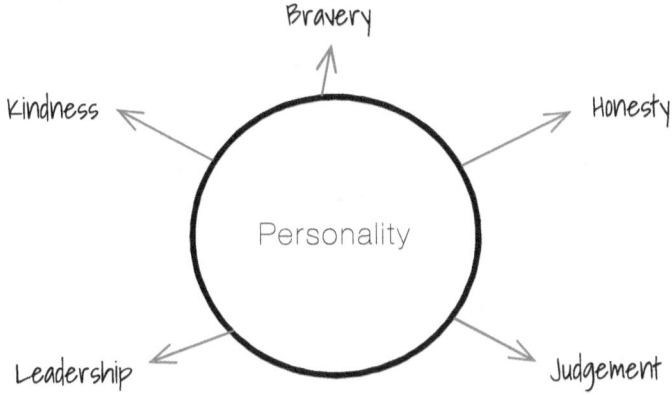

Are there any character strengths in your top five that surprise you? How do you think you currently use them as a mum? As a partner? At work? What might be the upsides and downsides of your character strengths?

My top character strength is Bravery. Before I became a mum, my strength of bravery would shine through during any major decision I would make. I was spontaneous and courageous. From going solo to Los Angeles on a whim at 23 to moving interstate alone and meeting someone from the internet I had never met at 25. I wouldn't even bat an eyelid. The downside of Bravery, of course, is risk exposure. But as a mum, I now find my bravery is used in conjunction with a bit of careful planning and forethought.

The VIA Institute on Character website is full of useful information on each character strength, including ways to use each strength every day, movies that feature main characters that demonstrate particular character strengths, and so much more.

Interests and Hobbies

Some of your hobbies and interests you had before you became a mother may still be relevant today, some you may have completely forgotten about, and others may mean nothing to you anymore. This is largely due to the personal growth you experience when you become a mother, which I mentioned previously.

Also known as Post-Traumatic Growth, highly stressful life events, such as becoming a parent, can sometimes create positive changes in anything from your self-perception, life direction, life appreciation, compassion for others and depth of connection to others. This growth can also affect the interests and hobbies you choose to pursue or let go of.

> **Meet Alicia**
>
> Since becoming a mother, Alicia has gradually lost interest in movies and television. She feels like she is no longer able to get 'sucked into' the plot of a movie or show because they seem too unrealistic or overly melodramatic.
>
> Alicia still has an interest in other hobbies, such as gardening and baking, which feel more practical in her life.

Everyone has specific interests and hobbies, and you usually choose them based on a few different personal reasons. Note down any hobbies and interests that spring to mind on your identity map as you read this section.

1. Think back to what you loved doing as a child. Chances are, you still have a lot of those same core interests. If it was tree climbing, maybe you can try wall climbing. If it was running through the bush behind your house, try hiking.

2. Think about the times where you enjoyed doing something so much that you completely lost track of time.

3. Literally, look around your home and see if there are any neglected hobbies that you started but haven't completed.

Values and Beliefs

Values are principles, standards or qualities that you hold in high regard. Beliefs, on the other hand, come from real experiences but are projected onto new experiences. Your values and beliefs both reflect who you are, guide the way you live your life and the decisions you make.

Examples of values: manners, friendships, courage, freedom, honour, hard work, generosity and individuality.

Examples of beliefs: 'Life is worth living', 'Love is worth the risks', 'Family always comes first' and 'Children are precious'.

Values and beliefs can change after kids, and these need to be brought to light. You then need to understand how they drive and influence your everyday decisions naturally.

Before motherhood, one of my biggest values in life was freedom. I hated the feeling of being locked or tied down by something, and many of the decisions around partners, money, careers and where I lived reflected this. Since becoming a mum, however, the sense of freedom I had is now more of a luxury, although this has morphed into a value for time. Twenty-four hours in the day seems much less when you have kids, and you always want to make every minute count!

- Are you aware of whether your values have changed after children?
- Do you have new beliefs based on your experiences as a mum?
- Are you connected with those values and beliefs, and make each decision with them in mind?

Occupation

As I mentioned earlier, so many women struggle to see themselves as more than a mum because we search for our identity in what we do, as opposed to who we are. We attach our identity solely to our job role or our daily activities. But you are more than what you do for a living.

Stay-at-home-mum vs. working mum, working to make ends meet vs. loving the job you're in, facing concerns about finances vs. career development vs. societal pressures... regardless of the position you find yourself in, your 'occupation' is actually an opportunity to express yourself in disguise!

When you express yourself, you are establishing the other parts of your identity (i.e. personality, interests and hobbies, values and beliefs, and talents and skills). In the meantime, you are also giving yourself purpose, self-confidence, value, and self-worth.

The occupational part of your identity is *not* about the specifics of what you do for a living. It's what you bring into what you do, and what that gives you in return.

If you are an accountant, are you great at; working with numbers? being in an office environment? working autonomously? helping people achieve financial peace-of-mind?

In return, does your accountancy work give you; skills you can use in your personal life? a sense of accomplishment at the end of the day? a thrill?

If you are a check-out operator, are you great at; working quickly and accurately under pressure? working with numbers? being friendly and polite to strangers? dealing tactfully with difficult people?

In return, does your work on the check-out give you; skills you can use in your personal life? a sense of connection to other people in the world? a thrill from helping others each day?

Look closely at why you do what you do. If it's not something you enjoy, or it gives you nothing in return, perhaps this is part of your identity that is yet to be defined. Chapter Eight of this book should be able to help you with this!

Talents and Skills

Talents are your naturally recurring patterns of thought, feeling or behaviour that you are essentially 'born with'. These may include leadership qualities, empathy, art, humour or listening.

Skills are learned over time, and often compliment your talents. These can include math, negotiation, decision making, writing, time management or computers.

Meet Anne

Anne has always had a talent for being able to effectively communicate with different people. Before she became a mother, Anne used to work as a call centre operator, where she learned sales skills to compliment her talent.

Anne strongly values direct communication, and believes that meaningful conversation creates trust. She always did very well at her job.

Now that Anne's children are of school-age, she is looking to get back into the workforce by applying for jobs that allow her to use both her talent and skills, as she knows these jobs will make her feel fulfilled.

Talents and skills are used to determine the way you go about things in life. When you are completing a task or activity that uses your talents or skills, it's the sense that things 'feel right' to you. This is because your talents and skills are being used in line with your values and beliefs.

Everyone has talents and skills — I guarantee you! Sometimes we just forget what they are, or haven't used them in a while. Go on, think hard and write some of them down on your map.

♥ ♥ ♥

So, now you should have the foundations of your identity; the woman you are *now*; the woman that exists in addition to 'Mum'.

Keep revisiting this chapter and your identity map as you read through the rest of the book. You may gain some new insights or ideas around who you have become since your motherhood journey began. This clarity will help you to make good decisions and positive changes in your life, for both you and your family.

When you figure out what you want from life, its then about plotting and scheming around your kids to make things happen — which later chapters can also help you with!

♥ ♥ ♥

Congratulations! You have made to the end of the first chapter. As a mum, I know what an achievement it can be to get this far in a book, let alone a book that has been written just for *you*. Ok, you may have had to read the chapter over a week's worth of train rides into work or during a week's worth of day naps, but guess what? You are already well on your way to making positive changes in your life.

As you complete this chapter and get ready to move onto the next, I want to reassure you that I don't intend for the actions in this book to be a burden. For everything discussed throughout the book to work for you, it may mean adapting things a bit, or simply saying to yourself 'I'm not ready to go there yet'.

If you do find parts of this book a bit overwhelming or revealing, consider talking about your discoveries over coffee with a friend or keeping a self-reflection journal.

In saying this, I'd like to encourage you on your journey with these three important, easy to do steps to start rediscovering who you are:

1. Create your Identity Map by drawing the five circles (P.I.V.O.T.) and start filling it in. If you start to see patterns or connections, draw lines to connect them!

2. Take the VIA Institute on Character Survey and reflect on your results, focusing on your top 5.

3. Keep adding to your Identity Map as you read through each chapter in this book.

2

Unload the Mental Load

Let me know if this sounds somewhat familiar...

"I wonder if Sam ate his lunch today? I gave him multigrain bread... I know he doesn't like it but he needs the extra nutrition. He eats way too much sugar... Oh, did he take his library books to school? I forgot to check. Shit, shit, shit... he didn't. Must take them up to the school... school! Right! I really need to get the school uniforms washed today or they'll have nothing to wear tomorrow... another thing to add to my list of things to get done. And he's been asking me for weeks to sign him up to footy, I really must do that tonight after the kids have gone to bed… Oh, and the school camp is next week — he has to pack his own bag. Oh God, he doesn't know how…"

This is the way our mother minds work; in overdrive! Every day, every waking hour. And it's almost impossible to switch off. I am always thinking about the things I need to get done on any given day; what I need to do that afternoon to make the night routine easier, or that night to make the morning routine run smoothly. I am always trying to remind myself of the day the bin needs to be put out, to bring the bin back in, the day my daughter needs to take her tennis racquet to school for her lesson, the day the washing needs to be done — the thoughts and personal reminders seem to never end!

Women are naturally multi-taskers, and this innate skill ramps up significantly after you become a mother. You are constantly trying to remember things you need to do, people you need to call, appointments you need to book, decisions you need to make… just to feel like you are in control of your life and are always ahead.

As mentioned in the previous chapter, you are the pivot of your family; the person they fundamentally depend on. And you depend on your brain power, A LOT! All these thoughts going around and around and around in your head are what is called 'mental load'. It's invisible, exhausting work that never ends, whether you are a stay at home mum, or a working mum. It is the constant worrying about daily activities. It is stress.

♥ ♥ ♥

We all want to be a Supermum. Able to handle anything that comes our way, always in control, feeling cool, calm and collected. We see another mum out there that appears to handle the mental load of motherhood well and we think "I can handle it all too!", or we start to feel inadequate by thinking things like "She has 3 kids and they always arrive at school on time in clean, ironed clothes and a homemade, nutritious lunchbox packed; I struggle to do those things with one child! I'm never going to be as good a mum as her…" That comparison stuff is toxic though, right?

The reality is, our bodies simply cannot handle this type of pressure, physically or mentally. That other mum may be very good at hiding the strain of her mental load (or maybe she has read this book!).

Have you ever noticed that when there is more going on in your life, and your mental load has increased, you suddenly start to feel 'off'? Maybe you catch a cold, a sore throat, you feel more anxious or down about things that don't normally bother you, your neck or back start to feel sore or your legs begin to cramp. For me, my sinuses will become painful, I lose full range of motion in my neck and my hips begin to feel stiff and sore. Not a place I want to be in for long!

Stress is stored in the muscles of your body, including the brain muscle. It is therefore unsurprising that mental load, or stress, can lead to a breakdown of your immune system and open you up to a variety of physical and mental illnesses.

Understanding the complex interrelationship between your mind and your body is a critical part of starting the process of destressing and controlling your mental load.

Your thoughts, feelings, beliefs, and attitudes can affect your biological functioning in both positive and negative ways. This whirlwind of things going on in your mind can be a positive force in your body that gives you the confidence, clarity, and motivation to be that Supermum! On the other hand, this same cocktail of emotions can leave you with one hell of a hangover! Either way, your mind can have a profound effect on how healthy your body is.

In reverse, what you do with your physical body can impact your mental state; again, positively or negatively. What you eat, how much you exercise, your posture, your quality of sleep… all of these physical actions can control the release hormones and other chemicals in your brain that affect your sense of calm and pleasure, alter your mood and reduce your experience of pain.

Trust me, this isn't just 'airy-fairy' rainbows and butterflies stuff, this is grounded in science! Your brain has a characteristic known as 'neuroplasticity'. This is how it adapts to your world based on your lifestyle, physiology, and environment. You are literally forming and re-forming your brain based on the choices you make and the habits you build on a day-to-day basis.

If some of these habits involve activities that strengthen the connection between your brain (mind) and your body, you are essentially teaching your brain how to *care for* your body, and your body how to look after your brain. All of this co-nurturing increases your resilience to stress and the ability to bounce back from excessively stressful events, when your mental load would normally overload.

As a mum that also suffers from the chronic pain condition, Fibromyalgia, regular practice of strengthening the mind-body connection is incredibly valuable and useful for me in my day-to-day life.

Okay, I get it, but how do I do it?

Fear not! You *can* feel like a Supermum by strengthening your mind-body connection. This chapter will explore many different ways you can release the stress built up in the muscles of your body and increase your resilience to mental overload. All approaches have been proven to be effective, however not all of them will suit every mum, so it is important to give each one a try in order to find which ones work best for you!

Body-Mind Approaches

Yoga and Tai Chi

Yoga has been practiced in India for several thousands of years. It is often defined as a practice 'that stills the fluctuations of the mind'. There are many schools of yoga, and not all involve the physical form of exercise that we tend to associate with the word 'yoga' here in Australia.

Physical yoga (Hatha) aims to strengthen the body by improving vitality, circulation, organ function, flexibility, and breathing. Yoga can include meditation (Dhyana), breath control (Pranayama) and chanting, as well as yoga posture (Asanas).

Tai chi is an ancient Chinese tradition that, today, is practiced as a graceful form of exercise. It involves a series of movements performed in a slow, focused manner and accompanied by deep breathing.

Similar to yoga, tai chi has three main components; exercise, meditation, and breathing. It is the combination of these techniques during practice that can strengthen the connection between your mind and body and create a focused, yet relaxed, state of being.

Creative Arts

Vincent Van Gogh once stated:

> *"I put my heart and soul into my work and have lost my mind in the process."*

Creating art puts you in a meditative state, which increases the integration of brainwaves and thereby strengthens the connection between your body and mind. You do not have to be a talented painter to experience this either.

Meet Heidi

Heidi is a mother of one and a full-time primary school teacher.

After reconnecting with the parts of her identity that she had forgotten since becoming a mum, Heidi wanted to get back into sewing, as this was a hobby she knew she loved when she was immersed in it.

Heidi made time weekly for her sewing and found that her stress levels reduced, and she had greater clarity and confidence in the decisions she made for herself and her family.

Immersive engagement in sketching, sculpture, music or dance — my personal favourite — to the point of losing a sense of time and place (read more about 'flow states' in Chapter Six) can also enhance the mind-body connection and create a feeling of contentment, regardless of how 'good' you are at it.

Breathing

If you've given birth (even if you've had a c-section, like me), you already know how the therapeutic use of breathing and breath awareness can affect your mind-body connection. You've probably seen or heard about someone breathing into a paper bag to help calm the body and mind in the event of a panic attack. It is a widely used technique to reduce pain and anxiety, as well as to assist with normal bodily processes involved in childbirth.

Incorporating breathing exercises into your busy day is one of the easiest strategies to improve your mind-body connection. I have taken to doing this several times a day to cope with my mental load — in the car, in the shower, just after a phone call, right before bed at night — whenever and wherever it is needed.

Spend just 15 minutes a day:

- sitting quietly and focusing on your breathing
- taking at least 3 deep breaths, exhaling slowly after each breath
- breathing in through just the left nostril, then breathing out through just the right nostril, repeating in reverse

Practicing these exercises regularly encourages the release of long-held tensions and unnecessary stress build up in your body and mind.

Progressive Muscle Relaxation

Progressive muscle relaxation involves the tensing and relaxing of specific muscle groups in your body, one at a time, and progressing throughout your entire body. This is my favourite de-stressing technique, as it also helps with symptoms of Fibromyalgia.

Before you begin, mentally scan your body from head to toe. Become gently aware of any area that feels tense.

Start with the muscles in your feet and legs, working up through each muscle group to your neck, shoulders, and scalp. Simply tighten each muscle group for at least 5 seconds until you really feel the tension, then release the muscles for 10 seconds.

This approach not only assists in the release of stress build up within the muscles of your body, but it also forces your mind to focus on something other than your never-ending thoughts about daily activities and to-do lists!

Massage

Massage therapy is commonly thought of as merely a healthcare alternative to ease or improve physical conditions, such as stiff joints or back pain. Although this may be true, massage also connects your body's feelings of comfort with your mind. The stimulation you feel from being touched:

- assists with the release of emotions stored in the muscles of your body
- provides sensations of security, relaxation and love
- naturally assists to reduce your stress and worry

This emotional release can increase self-awareness, giving you a clearer mind and new perspectives on different parts of your life, and inspire you to live a healthier life by making positive health changes.

But let's face it — getting a massage is all too often seen as indulgent and selfish. It is so easy for mums to dismiss the benefits of massage because of persistent feelings of guilt around taking time for yourself or spending money unnecessarily. But I'm here to tell you that having a session of massage therapy not only benefits you physically, mentally and emotionally, but it also benefits your loved ones because they no longer have to deal with a grumpy mummy, an angry mummy or a stressed-out mummy! Even if a professional massage is out of reach, having a friend or relative provide touch therapy can still provide the same benefits.

Mind-Body Approaches

Meditation

Meditation is cited as one of the most powerful approaches for restoring balance to your mind and body. In meditation, you experience a state of restful awareness in which your body is resting deeply while your mind is awake, though quiet. In this state, your mind can let go of old, unhelpful patterns of thinking and feeling and learns to heal itself.

Simple meditation practice can take all of 10 minutes following these four steps:

- S   Stop what you are doing
- T   Take a breath and pause
- O   Observe what is happening in your mind, body and external environment, without reacting
- P   Proceed with the mindful choice, decision, and action that results from this pause

Meditation is known to have numerous benefits on both the mind and body, including decreases in hypertension, heart disease, anxiety, depression, insomnia, and addictive behaviours. As little as eight weeks of meditation not only helps you to feel calmer but can also change various areas of your brain, including growth in areas associated with memory, empathy, sense of self and stress regulation.

Hypnosis

Enhancement of your mind-body connection through hypnosis can work in one of two ways. Firstly, hypnosis can be incredibly relaxing, which lowers the levels of stress in your body and mind and boosts your immune system.

Secondly, two important types of white blood cells significantly increase while you are actually *in* hypnosis, which also boosts your immune system and enhances your capacity to handle stress and mental overload.

Now, I know this might be right out of your comfort zone, but I encourage you to do some research on hypnotherapy first and find a reputable hypnotherapist; someone that you can trust and feel safe with is key in order to really reap the full benefits of hypnosis.

Self-Talk

It was Shakespeare that said:

> *"There is nothing either good or bad, but thinking makes it so"*

The truth of this can be seen when you look at your own self-talk patterns and the effect they are having on your body.

Self-talk is the voice you may sometimes hear in the background of your mind and can be positive or negative. Negative self-talk often involves words like 'can't', 'sorry', 'should', 'must', 'hope' and 'maybe.

If we go back to the mind of the mother at the start of this chapter, her thoughts are telling her that Sam has "been asking me for weeks to sign him up to footy, I really *must* do that tonight after the kids have gone to bed". Whilst her thought and intension is based on genuine motherly love, this is no 'gentle' reminder. By using the word 'must', she is commanding herself to adhere to a self-imposed, possibly unrealistic expectation. This immediately adds pressure and stress to her mind and body.

Consider this thought instead: "Sam has been asking me for weeks to sign him up to footy, I *will* do that tonight after the kids have gone to bed." Do you hear the difference? The thought is decisive, it's done and it's packed away. It simply becomes a definitive action, rather than a burdensome thought that continues to cycle in your mind.

Positive intentions reduce anxiety and stress and can result in positive outcomes.

Gratitude and Kindness

Along similar lines of self-talk is the practice of gratitude and kindness. Whilst these topics are covered in more detail later in this book, it is important to acknowledge their effects on the mind-body connection.

It's nothing new to hear that being kind and expressing gratitude to others can have positive effects on your mood and mental wellbeing, but did you know that they also boost your immune system?

Serotonin is a naturally occurring neurochemical that has a calming, mood-regulating and anti-anxiety effect. During an act of kindness or gratitude practice, your brain increases the production of serotonin, thereby improving your immune system.

To add to this, the hypothalamus, or the part of your brain that regulates a number of your bodily functions including your appetite, sleep, temperature, metabolism, and growth, actually activates when you feel gratitude, or display acts of kindness. So, we actually can't function without gratitude and kindness!

Check out Chapter 10 for easy, practical ways to integrate kindness and gratitude practices in your life.

♥ ♥ ♥

The approaches to strengthen your mind-body connection listed in this chapter are by no means exhaustive. Every day there are new techniques being created and new studies developed to test their credibility and usefulness.

Nevertheless, once you find an approach that works for you, make sure you create a ritual of practicing it in order to strengthen your mind-body connection and feel like a Supermum! Over time, your resilience to mental over-load will increase, as will your ability to release any stress stored in the muscles of your body.

♥ ♥ ♥

Here are three steps that you can action right now to start managing your mental load:
1. Reflect on your physical and mental responses to your mental load and overload. Start to get a better sense of

your early warning signs of being overstressed so you know when to intervene.

2. Choose just one approach to try over the next month. Endeavour to practice this approach regularly to truly identify whether it works for you and whether you can create a habit from it.

3. Start listening to your inner voice. If it tends to be more negative, write down some more positive alternatives and rehearse them like you would practice lines from a play.

3

Mindfulness Matters

I once arrived home after a 20-minute drive and was unable to recall much about the traffic or what I had heard on the radio. I felt as though I had been "lost in thought", yet I wasn't really able to recall what I thought about! It was like a small chunk of time was missing from my day that I had no control over; like I had been viewing someone else's activities instead of my own.

This is a great example of 'mindlessness'. Experiences like these feel very surreal to me; they even make me feel a little scared! In a state of mindlessness your thoughts wander, you're not paying attention to what's going on within or around you and you feel 'spaced out'.

In the previous chapter, we discussed the concept of 'mental load'; constant thoughts going around and around and around in your head, worrying and stressing about daily activities. Mindlessness is the next level of mental load; it's when the thoughts in your head start to become unfocused and jumbled because your brain is exhausted.

There is nothing wrong with mindlessness every now and then, as it's impossible to live every moment actively processing information in your brain. Long periods of mindlessness, however, can cause you to live your life on autopilot, without control over your thoughts, actions or responses when participating in daily experiences.

Mindlessness is especially hard to avoid as a mum; you're more easily run down; traditionally, due to lack of sleep, eating unhealthily or not engaging in enough physical movement.

But if you run on autopilot continuously, how many of your child's amazing milestones would you miss out on? Now *that* is a scary thought!

♥ ♥ ♥

I'm sure you've all heard the term 'mindfulness' floating around for a while now, but never fully understood what it involves. It's a concept that has existed for thousands of years, however, over the past decade, mindfulness has become quite popular in Western society thanks predominantly to Dr. Jon Kabat-Zinn, former Professor of Medicine at the University of Massachusetts Medical School, as well as developments in neuroscience and growing evidence supporting the benefits of mindfulness practice in today's complex world.

Mindfulness is deliberately being *present in the moment*, with *openness rather than criticism*.

To be mindful is to embrace the positive moments in our lives so we can get through the challenging ones.

There are 4 key benefits to practicing mindfulness techniques, which can lead to extensive personal growth, can help us be better parents to our children and avoid unnecessary (scary!) states of mindlessness.

Clarity and Awareness

Practicing mindfulness can provide clarity and increased awareness needed to face difficult situations or create change.

As a mum, I often feel like my mind is much like a shaken snow globe, clouded with the chaos of my thoughts and emotions. Practicing mindfulness helps me to settle everything down and focus on what is happening right here, right now. I am giving myself an opportunity to put everything on pause by just focusing on the sensations my body is experiencing in a given moment.

Over time, repeating mindfulness techniques can help you gain greater clarity and insight into your thoughts and emotions so you can step back from a situation, view it from different perspectives and take appropriate actions to improve or alter it.

Mindfulness practice can also lead to deeper insights into yourself, including your passions and values that motivate your actions and behaviours. You can use this information to discover more about who you are, make better choices and develop the steps needed to make those choices become reality.

Becoming more mindful was a key part of my journey to accepting who I had become after having my daughter, and knowing what actions I needed to take to start living a happier, more fulfilling life as a mother.

Calm and Patience

If you're naturally an impatient person, like me, or since becoming a mother your tolerance levels have reduced and the concept of calm has disappeared altogether, then mindfulness is probably one of the best practices you can undertake!

Mindfulness requires *and* fosters patience. You're bringing your attention back to the present, and to all the thoughts and emotions caught up in your mind. Regularly practicing mindfulness is developing your skill in patience, which can certainly be used in many situations as a mum!

I have found that whenever my engagement in mindfulness practice drops off, so too does my ability to handle life. I find myself flying off the handle at things that normally wouldn't bother me so much, like asking my daughter to clean up after herself for the umpteenth time, or getting upset over being stuck behind a slow driver. It's reflecting on these emotional reactions that help remind me to pick up my mindfulness practice.

With patience also comes a deeper sense of peace and calm; just like when a snow globe starts to settle. The more often you are mindful in life, the easier this sensation can be reached.

There is much research out there now that shows these same effects of calm and patience from mindfulness can also extend to controlling stress and anxiety symptoms. Mindfulness techniques help you to temporarily remove your mind from thoughts and emotions, including unhelpful ones. This then creates the space to replace them with more helpful ones.

Relationships

Mindfulness can improve all types of relationships you have with others through increased attentiveness, empathy and compassion.

Because mindfulness practice requires you to refocus your attention on the present, this attentiveness skill can be transferred to your connections with others. We all know that an inattentive or distracted friend or partner can be highly frustrating, causing friction between you both, right? With mindfulness, you become more present in your relationships, which builds intimacy and makes your relationships happier and more connected.

The non-judgemental component of mindfulness practice promotes self-acceptance, as well as the acceptance of others. Rather than simply avoiding people and situations, you can find it easier to see another person's point of view and develop empathy and compassion towards that person in the process.

When I first started attending mother's groups, both online and offline, I was overwhelmed with the amount of judgement some mothers would throw at one another over any decision another mother would make that didn't align with their own values and beliefs. Anything from breast versus bottle, co-sleeping, baby-led weaning, using the 'cry-it-out' method, returning to work early versus being a stay-at-home mum; there were so many critics!

At first, this put me off connecting with other mums. I was already my own worst critic; constantly judging and second-guessing my choices as a parent. But over time, with the ongoing cultivation of my mindfulness practice, I was able to see past the judgement, from both myself and other mums, and accept that this was sometimes part of being a mother in today's society. I could see the bigger picture; that mums out there were making choices based on their own knowledge, instincts, experiences and values — and that every decision was being made out of pure love for their children. Just as I was.

Concentration

Due to mindfulness techniques being embedded in openness and focus of the mind, it's unsurprising that long-term practice exercises your brain to increase your concentration levels and memory function.

Our brains are biologically wired to focus on negative experiences and events, therefore it is up to us to actively seek and remember the good times. The non-judgemental approach to mindfulness practice significantly reduces the amount of negative information you will recall, whilst improving your ability to remember more positive information, such as happy stories from your children and their life experiences, or a small personal win for the day, such as getting all green lights or through that pile of laundry.

♥ ♥ ♥

Before you begin to look at integrating more mindfulness into your life, it can be helpful to understand exactly how mindful you already are.

The Five Facet Mindfulness Questionnaire was developed as a holistic way of determining how mindful you are overall, as well as for the different elements of mindfulness i.e. observing, describing, acting with awareness, non-judging of experience and non-reactivity to experience (available at http://awakemind.org/quiz.php). There is no cut-off in the scoring that says you are or aren't mindful; the scores simply represent a spectrum of mindfulness (scores closer to 5 indicate more mindfulness; closer to 1 indicate less mindfulness).

Once you have completed the questionnaire, reflecting on your scores for each of the different elements of mindfulness can help guide your practice of mindful activities.

Meet Danielle

Danielle is a working mother of two.

In order to develop better patience, Danielle decided to practice more mindfulness, however she already felt she was a very mindful person.

After taking the Five Facet Mindfulness Questionnaire, Danielle found that her overall score was quite high, however her score for non-reactivity was fairly low.

Danielle found that her patience was always thin after a day at work, so she decided to engage in more mindful lunchtime activities at work, such as eating more mindfully by savouring her food and going on short, unintentional walks with heightened awareness of her surroundings.

After 3 months, Danielle found she was no longer emotionally-charged when reacting to challenges with her kids and felt calmer overall, both at work and when coming home.

On taking the questionnaire again, Danielle's score for non-reactivity had increased.

Mindfulness can be practiced in many ways and doesn't take much time; you're probably already doing it, to some extent. Some mindful activities may feel more natural than others, and some may take a little more time to get used to.

With practice, becoming mindful of yourself and your surroundings will come with less effort. Here are some wonderful examples of mindful moments for you to try:

- Next time you go for a walk, focus on *feeling your feet* on the ground as you take each step
- Take a *deep, full breath* in between phone calls and meetings at work
- Instead of tuning into the radio, *tune into the thoughts and feelings* you are experiencing as you drive
- Visit the beach or walk through a local park *without shoes* and focus on feeling the sand/grass/dirt as it connects with your feet
- Agree to *put your mobile phones away* next time you are out for coffee or dinner with friends and family
- *Pay attention* to your partner's facial signals
- *Step outside* your office or house during the day and spend a few minutes observing the smells, sounds, temperature, colours and interactions occurring naturally around you. You could even do this whilst waiting in line for a coffee or the bus.
- Spend one meal a day *savouring* each bite of food; experiencing its taste, smell, texture and the way it feels as it enters and travels through your body
- Colour-in with your kids

You can always encourage your children to try regularly practicing some of these techniques as well, which will motivate and remind you to do them too! This way, all of you are developing mindfulness skills, which, for your kids, will assist them as they travel through their life challenges at school, in social situations, puberty, and adulthood.

If you are looking to take your mindfulness exploration to a slightly deeper level, then the 'Self-Compassion Pause' exercise is perfect for you! Fair warning though; this exercise can be very challenging and confronting, as many mothers struggle with showing themselves compassion, even though we are ever-so-quick to extend compassion to others.

Adapted from the original exercise developed by psychologists and leaders in the field of mindfulness and compassion, Drs. Chris Germer and Kristen Neff, the 'Self-Compassion Pause' can be extremely empowering and liberating, as it can become a powerful tool to improve your confidence and resilience.

The Self-Compassion Pause

1. When you find yourself stressed out in a difficult situation, take a moment to pause
2. Reach up and touch your heart, or give yourself a hug if you are comfortable with that
3. Take a few deep breaths

4. Acknowledge that you are suffering and see if you can treat yourself with as much kindness as you would a dear friend or your child who was struggling

5. Say out loud 3 phrases of compassion:

    a. first, acknowledge your suffering — "This is really painful/difficult right now" or "Wow, I am really suffering right now!"

    b. second, acknowledge that all humans suffer and struggle — "Suffering is a part of being human"

    c. finally, offer yourself compassion — "May I love and accept myself just as I am" or "May I remember to treat myself with love and kindness"

6. Return to your daily activities, intentionally carrying an attitude of self-compassion and acceptance to your day

The last step may be the most difficult, it is also the most important one!

♥ ♥ ♥

Mindfulness is a relatively easy practice that, as a busy Mum, you can do, regardless of budget, occupation or personality type. Practicing mindfulness regularly can significantly enhance your quality of life, happiness, self-confidence, relationships, patience and peace of mind, among many other benefits.

While mindlessness can certainly have a place in a healthy, happy life, it can't hurt to try an activity that helps you become more aware of your body, your thoughts and who you are.

So go on — give yourself permission to pause and be present for whatever is happening at that moment, both inside you and around you. Over time, you might be surprised what you learn and how you change!

Three actions you can now take:
1. Take the Five Facet Mindfulness Questionnaire (a total of 39 questions) to get an idea of how mindful you currently are, and what part of mindfulness practice you might want to focus on.

2. Choose just one of the mindful moments suggested in this chapter, or come up with one of your own, to start practicing regularly each day.

3. Think about a mindfulness technique that you might like to start with your kids, which will work for both you and them.

NIKKI COX

4

Refill Your Cup

When you were pregnant, how often were you encouraged by friends, family or medical professionals to invest time and energy into taking care of yourself?

For some reason, this attitude, both in society and within the psyche of us as women, does not carry through to after your baby is born. It's almost as though the association between self-care and the mummy-to-be is cut along with the umbilical cord. *Snip!* And just like that, there is a disconnection. No longer does self-care mean good mothering, it suddenly means selfish mothering.

Although it is natural, normal and necessary to put your children's needs ahead of your own, more often than not Mums tend to over-action this message. Let's, however, put your job as a parent aside for just a moment.

Do you always put other people first?

Do you tend to define your worth by what you can do for someone else?

It is common for women to subconsciously internalise the message that we are expected to give and serve others. It is in our biological make-up to want to help others, especially once we give life to another human being, however *wanting* to give and giving out of *self-imposed expectation* are two very different things. While it's wonderful to make selfless gestures or give your time to good causes, you need to be wary of meeting other people's needs at the expense of your own *all* the time.

Even though I am consciously aware of my own innate tendency to want to please, help and give to the people around me, I frequently catch myself falling into the unhealthy cycle of putting the needs of others ahead of my own. Just the other night, I was caught up in the after-school routine rush — unpacking school bags, making lunches for the next day, serving dinner, washing dishes, getting washing off the line, folding and putting away said washing, cleaning up after dinner, stacking the dishwasher, changing nappies, bathing the kids... after getting through all of this, I realised I hadn't even sat down to eat my own dinner!

Neglecting your own self-care can lead to short-fuses, poor decisions, depression, anxiety and feelings of meaninglessness — none of which is good for anyone, let alone a Mum. Over a long period of time, it can even leave you feeling drained and passionless, without a sense of who you really are and what you enjoy.

As a mum, caring for yourself is a behaviour you have to train yourself in and commit to. And as you can see from my own example above, refresher courses in self-care practice are part of this commitment!

♥ ♥ ♥

Benjamin Franklin once said:

"When the well's dry, we know the worth of water"

When self-care is absent in your life, you can feel overwhelmed, exhausted and unappreciated by the people around you. Your sense of self-worth disintegrates, and before long you start to realise the need and value in reinvesting in your own wellbeing.

Practicing self-care restores the internal balance that is often disrupted as a result of endless giving; to your children, your partner, your work... and the list can go on. It's absolutely vital to learn how to consider your own needs against the needs of others, and how to feel good about caring for yourself as a Mum.

You've probably heard this old analogy, but here it is again to remind you of its importance:

You're on an airplane and an oxygen mask drops in front of you. What do you do? As we all know, the first rule is to put on your own oxygen mask before you assist anyone else. Only when we first help ourselves can we effectively be of help to others. If you can't breathe, you sure as hell can't help anyone else to breathe.

Caring for yourself is one of the most important things you can do for yourself, *and* for those around you. It provides you with the energy you need to keep up with your kids and give them the best of you. The moments you spend with your family will matter more, and things will appear to run more smoothly around you due to the positive shift regular self-care practice can have on how you see life events and handle them. This means feeling less impatience, anger, guilt, and frustration that we often project unconsciously during our interactions with our children and others.

But despite being such an important thing to do every day, nurturing yourself is also one of the easiest things to forget.

For the first few years after becoming a mother, practicing self-care for most of us is a bit like being on a rollercoaster; you are either really committed to it or it is completely absent. To add to this, the more children you have, the busier you are, the amount you are 'giving' to others increases, and the more absent self-care tends to become.

Meet Miriam

Miriam is a stay-at-home mum of three; two of which she home-schools.

Miriam was feeling very lost and passionless. Her life completely revolved around her children, and she never took any time for herself.

As a result, Miriam started to resent her husband for the way she was feeling; she felt trapped within her own life. Wanting to make a change, Miriam started to investigate hobby classes she might enjoy, and decided to talk to her husband about how he and their eldest daughter could support her in making time each week to attend these classes.

Miriam now feels much more confident, happy and validated in her life.

Looking after yourself often gets pushed more and more to the side, until you become chronically stressed, you've gained weight, you're completely burnt out or you've developed even more serious health issues, such as depression, diabetes or obesity. The ironic part is that we usually sacrifice our self-care so we can get more things done, however all this does is leave you feeling frazzled, resentful and overwhelmed with less capacity and resilience to get everything done due to running on an 'empty cup'.

This chapter is going to provide you with the mindset shift you need to start seeing self-care as something worth investing in every day. More than this, I'm also going to show you how self-care can actually work in the busy life of a Mum.

♥ ♥ ♥

To function and thrive, we need to feel well, do well and be well, and a fundamental part of this is self-care. Simply put, self-care is about nurturing your mind and thoughts, your body and physical health, and your emotions. But the concept of 'self-care' has become a bit of a buzz word on social media these days, with many misconceptions about what it truly is and what it looks like. Let's start by clarifying what self-care actually is, and is not.

Defining Self-Care

It is very important to understand that self-care is essentially made up of two different categories of activities. Firstly, there are your 'basic needs'; things that are important predominantly to your physical wellbeing, such as bathing, eating, brushing your teeth and hair, and being clothed.

Secondly, there are your 'cup-fillers'; activities that you enjoy, that you consider fun, make you feel happy, fulfilled and inspired.

Sometimes these self-care activities can cross-over — a long hot shower can be extremely enjoyable and is also important for our health. With that said, it is perfectly ok if some days all you can manage is your basic needs. I have certainly had many days where I was either sick, rushed or simply caught up in the chaos of being a mother and a homemaker that getting dressed, brushing my hair and making it out of the house felt like a true achievement.

Finding opportunities for deeper self-care activities from the second category, however, is a critical part of achieving and maintaining wellness. It's about treating yourself like you love yourself and acting like your needs and enjoyment matter just as much as anyone else's. Ultimately, taking the time to give yourself what you need leads to greater happiness, calm, emotional resilience, clarity, motivation, and energy.

Self-care activities that fill your cup look different from Mum to Mum, and they don't always need to be done alone or without your kids. In addition, if scented bubble baths and meditation bring on a major case of the eye-rolls (like they do for me!), then you probably won't feel replenished by doing them. Don't like yoga? Don't do it! There is no wrong or right way to 'do' self-care. Remember the old K.I.S.S. principle (Keep It Simple, Stupid)? It applies to your self-care choices too. Acts of self-care could include anything from taking a nap to exercising, spending time with friends, catching up on a favourite TV show, getting your hair done, taking a bubble bath, watching a sunset or reading a book.

Feelings around Self-Care

Now that you understand what self-care truly is, and what it can look like, let's address the elephant in the room: guilt.

Grab your journal, or a piece of paper, and a pen. Draw a line down the centre of the page, so you have two columns. I want you to look at the past week and, in the left-hand column, list down *all* of the things you did for your children; you might have hosted play dates, taken them out for lunch, went on bike rides, played at the park, trips to the library, took them to sports, school, the zoo etc.

Now, in the right-hand column, list down the things you did for *you*.

Your first list is surely longer than your second, and probably always is. Whether you're a working, studying or stay-at-home mum; whether your children are of pre-school, primary school or high school age; the numbers don't lie. You are ensuring that the needs and enjoyment of your kids are being met, but are yours? There is *nothing* to feel guilty about.

Still not convinced? How about looking at it this way. When you don't make time to take care of yourself, you are saying that everything else you do is more important. The washing is more important. Work is more important. Cleaning is more important. Really?? Do you think these things would get done (or get done well) if you became sick or burnt-out from chronic stress as a result of running on 'empty'? No way! There is *nothing* to feel guilty about.

Once in a while, I still get the 'guilts' over doing something for myself. It can sometimes take a physical stress reaction, such as a migraine or back pain, or an angry outburst to realise that my self-care practice has been neglected, and suddenly I realise there is no longer a reason for feeling guilty. I am no good to the people around me when I am stressed, angry, tired or in unnecessary pain. If I'm not happy, my kids aren't happy. These are strong reminders, for me, that there is no justification for my guilt over self-care.

Say it with me now; "there is *nothing* to feel guilty about!"

Sustainable Self-Care

If you already practice some self-care, do you do it *regularly?* Regular, small pockets of time for self-care is far better for a mum than occasional big actions such as a massage or even a weekend away. This is the notion of 'Sustainable Self-Care'.

Firstly, sustainable self-care is scheduled. Have a weekly planner on your fridge that marks out self-care time for either you or you and your partner. Use it to also map out regular weekly commitments for the kids (there is much more on this in the next chapter).

Secondly, it is short but sweet. Fifteen minutes to yourself every day is, in fact, more beneficial than an hour to yourself once a month. With 15 minutes totally for yourself, you can meditate, take a short walk, drink a cup of tea that is still hot, sing or dance to a couple of your favourite songs or read a chapter of a book in the garden.

Lastly, sustainable self-care is a commitment to constant work in progress. It is so easy to let the madness of motherhood get the better of you. There are always so many things to juggle, and it is incredibly easy to let self-care be the first ball that gets dropped.

As long as you honour your commitment to regular, sustainable action, you will feel like a much happier woman.

In The Moment Self-Care

When was the last time you asked yourself "What do I need *right now?*"

This question can help you practice 'in the moment' self-care, which is essentially a brief reconnection with yourself to quickly identify and satisfy a need that is going unnoticed and unmet.

It's extra important to practice self-care when you have lots of outside stressors, you feel unwell or run down, you are feeling overwhelmed or you notice your inner voice is putting your down. If you can take less than a minute to ask yourself this question in these situations, you might uncover the need for:

- a quiet moment to think
- something to eat or drink
- getting outside for some fresh air
- a hug or physical connection
- sleep or rest
- a change of scenery
- someone to talk to
- some help
- a few deep breaths
- a change in perspective

This question is a habitual part of how I look after myself each day, and can totally change what happens next for me; from a decision to be made, to a conversation with someone, to how I spend my next 5 minutes or the rest of the afternoon. It's a highly practical, easy-to-do strategy that, over time, gets easier to integrate into your busy life as a Mum, and can have a huge effect on your approach to self-care.

♥ ♥ ♥

Self-care is *not* selfish, *not* self-indulgent and *not* a luxury; it is certainly not something to be guilty about.

Self-care is an essential part of your being. It helps give us the energy to give and give and give to our children. It helps preserve our patience and sanity. It helps us feel valued in the world and creates a deeper sense of connection and joy within our family unit.

If that's not enough, remember that your kids are watching everything you do. The only way your children are going to learn about their own self-care is from your actions. When it comes to how you treat yourself, children learn how to look after themselves, treat themselves, spend money on themselves and love themselves from what they see you, and other adults they love and admire, do.

So start shifting the way you see self-care; what it is, what it looks like and what it means to you and your family. Looking after yourself and regularly refilling your cup is the most critical step to living a happier, balanced life as a woman with children.

Three actions you can now take:
1. Throughout all of the chapters in this book are ideas for self-care activities; whenever one 'sparks' something in you, add it to a list that you can refer back to at any time.
2. Write the following on a sticky note and place it somewhere you can read it daily: "I *am* important, looking after myself is *essential* to happy family life and I am *committed* to doing something for *me* every single day."
3. Create a reminder to regularly start asking yourself "What do I need *right now*?" in order to increase self-awareness of your needs, and develop your own healthy self-care habit.

NIKKI COX

5

It's Time for You

As we explored in the previous chapter, mums often get visited by guilt. You can feel guilty when the house isn't clean, guilty when you are too tired, too sick or too broke to take the kids out, guilty when you don't feel like having sex with your partner, guilty for working, guilty for not working, and guilty whenever you take time away from your family to look after yourself.

I often work with mums who are also battling with the guilt of not being able to do it all, and I can wholeheartedly relate to what they are going through. I would feel like I was failing as a mum, a partner, a housekeeper, a work colleague, and a friend. I would second guess every decision I made;

never trusting that I had made the right one. I would tell myself that I could do better and just needed to keep pushing or try harder. The guilty feelings were then compounded by constantly being told to take the time to look after me. My inner voice would respond with something like: 'Seriously? When do you think I can fit *that* in too? I don't *have* the time to spend on me!'

When was the last time you used the phrase "I don't have time"? I'm willing to bet it was recently and is used quite often.

While motherhood is definitely one of life's greatest joys, it can also be one of life's most time consuming and overwhelming jobs. It can be difficult enough balancing your responsibilities and quality time with your family, thus making time for yourself is never a top priority.

What's more, the odds of having spare time to yourself always seem completely unfeasible. Simple activities such as enjoying a cup of coffee while reading a magazine or scrolling through social media are no longer basic routines. Embarking on social endeavours, like a last minute night out on the town with your mates or an intimate dinner with your partner, are often cast aside, as these pleasures can be more of a hassle than they're worth.

Time certainly becomes a luxury when you are a parent, but that doesn't mean you can't still have time for yourself.

♥ ♥ ♥

There are a lot of times in your day where there are more demands on you than what you can possibly do. You're cooking, cleaning, preparing, planning, taking and making calls, checking and double-checking, reading, signing, fixing, refereeing… you only have two hands, but sometimes it feels like you need six.

Over time, every mum develops their own way of prioritising what needs to happen at that moment. A pattern I often see, however, is that you tend to put yourself lower down on that list of priorities. If and when you *ever* put yourself first, there is a huge surge of guilt that follows, which reduces your ability to enjoy your 'me' time, so you give up on it and go back to doing something more 'productive', which just makes you tired and in need of some 'me' time all over again!

As a mum, it seems like you have such little time, but so much guilt — it almost feels like a cruel joke.

From the moment your baby is conceived, your entire being was probably flooded with this feeling of 'Mummy Guilt'. During pregnancy alone, I could have filled a wheelbarrow with all of the guilt I placed on myself. I ate too much ice cream, not enough vegetables, and I even drank a can of soft drink or two (or six). It only got worse when my daughter was born. The guilt consumed me on a daily basis; it may have come and gone in waves, but it was always there.

Statistically speaking, 'Mummy Guilt' is a universal feeling. Across a multitude of studies, all mums have reported feeling guilty about some aspect of parenting. Stay-at-home-mums and working mums alike say they suffer from equal amounts of guilt. If you let it become all-consuming, however, guilt can get the best of you. When your guilty feelings are prominent, it can be difficult to think straight, can drain you of energy and make you reluctant to enjoy life. Guilty feelings can also lead to resentment towards people or situations.

According to Dr. Guy Winch, psychologist, and author of 'Emotional First Aid', you can't live a completely guilt-free life, but it can be kept at a manageable level.

As you read through this chapter, you will explore the foundations of 'Mummy Guilt'. Understanding what drives the overwhelming guilt we all experience as mums will allow you to take control of your feelings and be more comfortable with making decisions to invest in *you*. I will also show you how to prioritise yourself amongst everything in your life, and give you practical ways to make 'me' time a reality.

Sound good? Great! Then let's start by taking your guilty feelings down a notch or two.

Overcoming Guilt

Now, most mums are happy and, of course, you love your children, but this section isn't about that. Although it can be problematic at times, the fact that you feel guilty makes you a better parent and means you care.

Guilt can come from a variety of sources, but for mums, there is usually one key source: trying to be *perfect*.

Let me be blunt; perfection is an impossible goal. There is no such thing as a perfect parent; some degree of falling short is to be expected. And feelings that come from this, such as guilt, are a sign that something needs to change. But, as previously mentioned, it is unrealistic to simply 'stop' feeling guilty altogether.

Instead of trying to ditch it completely, there are a few things you can do to harness and channel your inner guilt.

1. Stop comparing yourself to other mums. The time could be better spent enjoying time with your children… or at least folding the laundry.

2. Go ahead and 'drop some balls', and laugh about it as they fall. Where is it written that your role as a mum is to juggle a huge number of balls, and to do it continuously and perfectly? You can't. You won't. Why beat yourself up over it?

3. Give yourself a little self-praise each day. Before you go to sleep tonight, think about 2 or 3 things that you achieved during the day. Even if it's just that you spent 15 minutes playing with your kids without checking your phone, or you didn't burn dinner during the witching hour.

4. Trust yourself, listen to your intuition and don't look back.

Some days truly feel like a waste; unproductive and like you've been chasing your tail. Focusing on your day in this way is when the guilt creeps in, and that little voice inside your head starts criticising your choices and abilities. But I'm willing to bet you do more than you think!

I have created a habit now for when I start to feel this way; I reflect, even part way through the day, on everything I have achieved. All of a sudden it might be 10 am and I wonder how that happened! Well, if I think about it, I prepared breakfast, put on a load of washing, packed school bags, unstacked the dishwasher, cleaned up after my kids, got myself and the kids dressed, did my hair, did my daughter's hair, spent 20 mins playing with my son and chatting with my daughter about her day ahead, got my kids to school, did some grocery shopping, put the shopping away and responded to a handful of emails. All before 10 am — wow! Hang on, I'm amazing! Sure, there are things that still need doing, but I have nothing to feel guilty about.

Prioritising You

We often get stuck in the cycle of getting consumed by all the demands in our life. The reality is the housework is always going to be there. You will always come across tasks that need to be completed and times where it often feels like it all needs top priority.

Ever been short of time, madly racing around and then something else really urgent pops up and suddenly you've got to fit that in too? What happens? Often you get it all done. You manage to fit it in, or you let something not so important fall by the wayside. This is because you made that urgent thing a priority.

Having the time to do something (like 'me' time) is never about time, it's about priorities. If you are not making yourself a priority, you won't make time for you. You'll keep putting yourself last and justify it by saying "Oh, I didn't have time for that". But it's not because you don't have time. We always have time. It's because you didn't make it a priority.

In the previous chapter, you read a lot about why making time for self-care is so important; for you, for your kids, for your home life... for everyone around you. Shift your priorities and you will find the time.

An important lesson to learn as a mum is not to fill up your life with things until you have made a space for what matters most.

In your journal, or on a piece of paper, write the headings: Rocks, Pebbles, and Water. Rocks represent the most important things in your life. Pebbles are somewhat important and Water are not very important at all.

Now, I want you to write the following under whichever heading you think it belongs, *according to their importance to you.*

- Family
- Sports and clubs
- Time on the internet
- Friends and other relationships
- Work
- Household chores
- School or other educational activities
- Time with God
- Movies/TV
- Personal skill development
- Physical exercise
- Self-care activities

Thinking about the things you placed under the 'Rocks' heading, do you believe you are spending the majority of your time well on these?

In what ways are you wasting time in your life on unimportant things (the stuff listed under 'Water')?

It is important to note that you may have differing opinions from other mums, and that's ok; there is no right or wrong answer here. For example, spending time on the internet may seem frivolous to you, but for me, it's a huge part of connecting with my family, who all live interstate. This exercise is designed to help you see, visually, the distance there might be between what your value priorities are, and what you actually prioritise day to day.

Finding 'Me' Time

Let's now look at the steps you can take to make 'me' time a reality.

1. First, decide that you deserve some time to yourself each day.

Stop feeling guilty for taking time out for you, and realise in the long run, it's a win-win for everyone (as discussed in Chapter Four). When you are tired, stressed out and pulled in too many directions, it is hard to give your best you.

Remember, time for yourself is not selfish — it's a necessary dimension of self-care.

Making this decision won't necessarily mean that self-care all of a sudden becomes a bed full of roses — it may still feel uncomfortable. It's kind of like the discomfort of taking sickly sweet cough medicine when you're sick; you know it's good for you, so you sit with the discomfort anyway. This feeling might be the same when you start carving out time for yourself too. Trust that it's good for you, even if it doesn't *feel* good at the moment.

2. Now, decide how best to spend your 'me' time.

How each of us chooses to spend free time is an individual thing, but try not to get caught up in wanting the perfect version of 'me' time as this defeats the purpose of having 'me' time in the first place, and cycles back to feelings of guilt.

If you had an extra 15 minutes, a half hour or an afternoon, what would you do to make yourself feel rejuvenated, relaxed and happy? Perhaps you could refer to the list of self-care activities you may have started at the end of Chapter Four.

3. Next, evaluate the things that are wasting your time each day.

Do you check your emails constantly and end up spending more time on your computer than you planned? Do you answer personal calls in the middle of your workday? Do you run to the supermarket daily to pick up dinner rather than planning in advance and shop once? Are you spending a large amount of time on things from your 'water' list, and not enough on your 'rocks'?

If this sounds like you, you may need to take the time to organise your responsibilities, and you will gain more free time than you can imagine.

> Meet Rachel
>
> Rachel is a single mum of three who was desperate to find some time for herself, but couldn't see how it was possible. Between commuting for school drops-offs and pick-ups, to and from work, coordinating extra-curricular activities, running a household and getting enough sleep each night, Rachel's schedule seemed completely full.
>
> Once Rachel had the opportunity to sit down and map out her daily events, she realised that her commuting activities could be made simpler and more efficient by using different routes, car-pooling opportunities and better timing.
>
> Rachel gained back up to 30 mins each morning, which she could now spend on herself.

The **next two steps** are hard ones for a lot of mums:

4. Learn to say "no" to requests to do things that you don't really want to, don't value or don't bring you satisfaction and joy.

Respect your precious time and energy by spending it on tasks, or with people, that matter most to you. You aren't doing yourself any favours by overscheduling your days and taking time away from necessary self-care and development.

Just keep your response simple and be firm and direct. If you need to, consider a compromise, but make sure you stay true to yourself. And know that it's ok if the other person initially feels upset or disappointed; their feelings are not within your control and remind yourself that you are looking out for you.

5. Ask for help.

Reach out to your partner, your mum, mother-in-law or a good friend. Just ask! You are worthy of getting a little help so that you can look after yourself. Better yet, if they are old enough, ask the kids to help you get things done, so you can have time just for you later. Everyone will benefit from the experience all around.

I know, I know… whenever others have 'helped out' in the past, you often think to yourself that "I could have done it better". I personally struggle with this step the most. But when you do everything yourself all the time, you can sometimes leave other people feeling inadequate or less confident. Once you let go of your need to control tasks and situations, it will actually empower others to step up, take ownership and responsibility for themselves, and you get to kick back and put your feet up for a bit!

6. Lastly, at the beginning of each week, take a few minutes to designate specific time slots for all that must be accomplished — including at least 15–20 minutes for "me" time per day.

Treat your personal time like you would any other appointment and make it non-negotiable, then do something (or nothing) that completely lets go of responsibilities and releases your mind, allowing you to be alone with your thoughts.

♥ ♥ ♥

Motherhood can be all-consuming. Trying to carve out a little bit of 'me' time is a great way to gain perspective. When you're having those guilty feelings, treat them as an invitation to change something and, more specifically, to prioritise your own needs more than you currently do. Once you begin prioritising the enjoyment of your parenting experience, you will want to create even more ways to do so.

When you're in the moment it's easy to beat yourself up over things that don't really matter in the long run. You will survive, so will your kids, the world will keep turning and tomorrow is a new day.

♥ ♥ ♥

Three actions you can now take:

1. Fill-in a simple weekly planner template (Calendarpedia has lots to choose from www.calendarpedia.com) to reflect on the way you are spending your time each day.

2. Practice asking for help, where you can.

3. Make a 15–20 minute, non-negotiable appointment with *you* in your diary for at least 3 days this week.

6

Take Control of Your Happiness

Do you often find yourself getting annoyed at the people around you, or irritated by the things other people do?

Are you noticing that, as the years pass, your tolerance levels are reducing and you get irritated and angry at extremely trivial things, such as someone leaving a big gap in the line, someone chewing food loudly nearby or someone in your house not replacing the empty toilet roll?

Can't pin down what's bugging you so much?

We don't always notice when there's something on our minds. When you're stressed out or not satisfied with life, but not sure why, your mind focuses on all the little things that annoy you — that you probably wouldn't normally notice. When there's a lot on your mind, you have less room to handle other people's problems or the way they act, and you can be a lot less forgiving.

This is a normal experience from time to time, but it can cause a lot of grief when you're being hard on friends, workmates or family for something small. A little kid is bothering you on the airplane; a man is talking loudly into his phone; a lady asks you the same question twice at the post office — these are all small annoyances in the big scheme of things, and they don't matter. But when you are feeling overwhelmed, unhappy and unfulfilled in life, all of sudden they *do* matter.

I am definitely someone who gets frustrated easily. Stresses in life creep up on me and all of a sudden I'm annoyed at every red light I get, can't wait patiently in a queue at the supermarket or start focusing on my mistakes or faults instead of my accomplishments. On my worst days, even my husband coughing or clearing his throat can irritate me immensely!

And loving your children doesn't mean they won't get under your skin sometimes too. Making a total mess, insisting on reading the same book over and over again, answering every single question with "No", clinging to you, throwing tantrums, refusing to sit still... it can drive you bonkers!

Getting some perspective, letting things go and not sweating the small staff keeps us sane, stops us losing otherwise valuable relationships and can greatly improve your happiness and quality of life.

♥ ♥ ♥

Leading researchers in Positive Psychology believe that we all have a 'set point' (or where your mind and body like to be) for happiness, much in the same way you have a set point for your body weight. That is, regardless of what you do, and however much you fluctuate, your mind and body tend to find their way back to a certain level of happiness, or weight.

Half of your happiness set point is said to be determined by factors that relate to your disposition; that is, your inherent nature to behave or feel in a particular way, which arguably cannot be permanently changed. This has usually been shaped by your heredity, family of origin and life experiences.

Another 10% is determined by your circumstances (e.g., socioeconomic status), and the remaining 40% is determined by your intentional activity or the things you deliberately do to lift your mood and spirits, e.g., exercise, spending time with loved ones, listening to music.

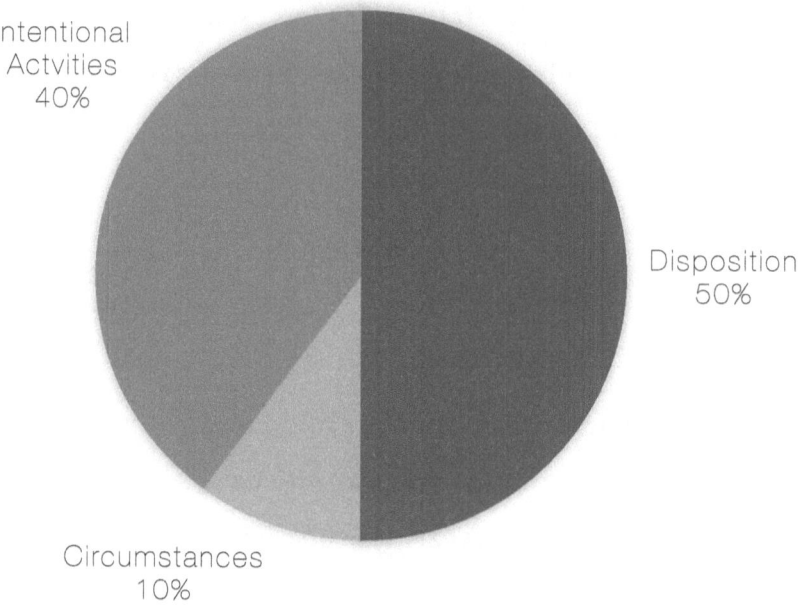

So, while there may not be much you can do about the 60% that is out of your control, you can do something about the remaining 40%, and actually, have quite a bit of influence over being happy in life.

You've probably heard the saying "Happiness is a journey, not a destination", and wiser words have not been spoken with regards to living a happier, less-stressful life. The goal is not to become happy, but rather to seek happiness as part of a way of life. And we all know that a Happy Mum = Happy Kids!

There are many theories on what happiness truly is, and how to achieve it, however the most prominent of these comes from the founder of the positive psychology movement himself, Dr. Martin Seligman. Seligman believes that the pursuit of true happiness in life must have a multifaceted approach (you can read more about his PERMA model here: https://positivepsychologyprogram.com/perma-model/).

You need to:

- experience positive emotions
- fully engage in the activities of life (work, play, relationships, parenting, etc.)
- have positive, supportive relationships with others
- seek meaning in life through broader perspectives on worries and issues, and
- have goals and challenges in life to strive for and reach a sense of accomplishment

Now, don't get me wrong. Negative emotions are beneficial to living a happy life too. Negativity is a very natural and important psychological resource. All emotions, both positive and negative, serve to motivate both your thoughts and actions; they are psychological measurements of your wellbeing and tell you when you are more or less happy.

There are moments where allowing yourself to acknowledge and experience negative emotions can help you achieve better results in your life, work and relationships. This is because negative emotions, in particular, prompt us to act upon our current circumstance and generate positive changes. You don't change because you are feeling good. You change when you feel something is wrong; when something is making you unhappy and you can't bear it any longer. Negative emotions motivate us to act towards change, and feeling constantly frustrated or unhappy are clear signs that you need to make changes in your life in order to take back control over your happiness

Reducing stress and mental load using the activities suggested in previous chapters is a great place to start gaining control over negative feelings of irritation and lack of satisfaction in life. The better you get at dealing with stress, the less something will appear to be an issue, due to the clarity and insight you gain from stress release.

This chapter will build on these strategies by providing you with ways to tackle annoyances head-on and create every-day experiences that can boost your mood, increase your happiness and inject more fun into your life on a regular basis.

So let's ditch the unwarranted frustration and begin your happier journey through motherhood!

Reducing Irritation

Irritation can be a great gift if you use it to understand more about yourself. When you are next feeling annoyed or frustrated, I want you to ask yourself these 4 questions:

1. What am I feeling?

Annoyed! Look at how you are feeling and own it. This means you understand that you are the one having the feeling; no one is making you annoyed. You are choosing to react to what is happening by feeling annoyed.

2. What does that feel like in my body?

Feel your annoyance in your body, outside of the confusion in your mind. What does feeling annoyed do to your body? When I am annoyed, my head feels hot, my neck and shoulders become extremely tense and my heart starts racing. Just breathe and feel.

3. What am I feeling annoyed about?

Emotions of all kinds can flood over us, and sometimes we don't even know what the trigger is. Take a moment to see what it was that you reacted to with annoyance. Is it to do with them, or you? Is it just one thing, or a culmination of things?

4. How much does it really matter?

Think about why the thing you feel annoyed about truly matters to you. Was there perhaps an inner need for order, gratitude or recognition that wasn't being met, that led to you feeling annoyed? A pet annoyance for me is other drivers that don't use an indicator when turning. This is connected to my inner needs for courtesy from others and to feel safe when on the roads. But how much does this truly matter? Although there is a small possibility of an accident being caused, in the grand scheme of things it matters very little.

Taking the time to stop within the heat of irritation and reflect on your feelings using these questions is a useful way to cope. Follow up with:

- breathing deeply from your diaphragm to reduce the amount of stress that your body is feeling
- asking yourself "What do I get out of being annoyed?"
- assume the best, instead of assuming that the annoying person is *trying* to annoy you; perhaps they don't know how they are coming across to you or are going through something personal
- remind yourself that annoyed people are annoying

You can't change things about the world, but you *can* change how you react to it. Take a leaf from Elsa's book in 'Frozen' and try to let go of how people *should* act and what people *should* do. While expecting others to be fundamentally decent is a worthy idea, it can cause unhealthy annoyance and unhappiness.

For a bit more perspective, there's a silver lining to the things your kids do that drive you nuts too, so remind yourself (as I do regularly!) of these the next time you're ready to rip your hair out:

- Young kids who make a total mess with their food are able to learn the words associated with those foods faster and more accurately.
- The repetition of reading the same book over and over again (or singing the same song, or playing the same game) is helpful for speech development; hearing the same words and phrases over and over again helps to cement them into a growing vocabulary and appropriate grammar.
- That stubborn and uncooperative "No!" you're so tired of hearing is your child asserting his or her independence and developing a healthy concept of self.
- Bottling up anger and frustration isn't good for anyone, children included. Your child is at the beginning stage of a journey we're all on: to learn healthy skills and coping mechanisms for dealing with difficult emotions instead of just repressing them.

- Research has found that there's a good chance the child who squirms during meals or runs laps around the house before bedtime won't struggle to maintain a healthy weight later in life.

The Importance of Play

Your self-esteem is based on your self-concept, where the self-concept is 'how I see myself', and self-esteem considers 'how I feel about how I see myself'. Having positive self-esteem adds to your quality of life and general well-being through positive emotions and decreased stress. There is also a strong connection between positive self-esteem and happiness, as well as negative self-esteem and depression.

Many mothers have low self-esteem for a variety of reasons, however, regular participation in leisure and play-based activities (i.e. activities that are voluntarily done to spend away from stress, such as sport, gardening, reading, walking, baking, etc.) can increase your self-esteem levels.

'Playing' is a form of self-nourishment, but we often see it as unproductive, time-wasting, selfish or just for kids. The truth is, play is just as critical to adults as it is for children, for a balanced, happy, fulfilling life. But play is more than just fun activities; it's an attitude to transform the way you see things. It's doing anything in life with humour, goodwill, compassion, openness and with a light touch and heart, whilst also being respectful.

Briefly think about your current level of self-esteem, then consider the amount of leisure or play-based activities you participate in each week. Do you believe there is a connection?

> **Meet Lee**
> Lee is an introverted mum of a special needs child, and has always been a naturally serious person. She is pretty rigid, and always wants things done a certain way. But Lee knew this way of living was constantly building up stress and anxiety in her body.
> Lee would see other people who were always joking and playing as inauthentic and silly. She also saw that these people seemed happy, carefree and had strong connections with others.
> In an effort to increase her happiness, Lee decided to play more in life, especially with her son. She started watching funny movies, playing music more often in the house, dancing — even splashed about in the rain on a wet day.
> Over time, Lee became more light-hearted towards the routines in her life and started to seek out regular opportunities to have fun.

As your self-esteem levels increase, this will improve the view you have of yourself, which will then increase the likelihood that you will actively seek leisure and play activities. So the more you do these activities, the easier it becomes to maintain the momentum!

It's important to remember that a leisure or play activity must be satisfying to you, or you may become bored, which can have the opposite effect and lower your self-esteem. Also, increases to your self-esteem as a result of a leisure activity usually plateaus after three months, so remember to apply some variety to the way you spend your 'me' time.

Go With the Flow

Do you ever get so deeply involved in something that nothing else seems to matter and you lose complete track of time? What are you doing? Is it during leisure or play-based activity? Or something else?

The experience of "flow" (also referred to as 'in the zone') is being fully engaged with whatever you are doing; actions are performed with little conscious effort, time appears to slip away and you no longer feel separate from the activity but rather completely merged with it.

Flow can happen anywhere, at any time. It usually accompanies a personally challenging activity that requires some skill to perform. Many people experience flow at work, despite most of us disliking work or wanting to work less. Others experience flow whilst participating in hobbies, sports or artistic pursuits; even whilst driving the car!

Whilst the frequency of flow experiences can vary from person to person, the ability to stay absorbed and interested in our daily experiences is fundamental to living a happy and fulfilling life, and can also help to build your self-esteem.

The best place to start creating more flow-like experiences is by reviewing a previous experience. You are your own best teacher, and drawing from previous flow experiences will create familiarity with the feelings experienced at that time, thereby building your self-confidence.

Spend a few minutes thinking back to a previous time and place when you were feeling fully engaged with whatever you were doing.

What do you see? Who else is there? What can you taste/smell/hear? How do you feel? How long do these feelings last?

Now, give your experience a name to file it away, much like you do with computer files. For example, you might choose to name it according to the place where you were, or a name that epitomises the experience for you.

When you want to use these images and sensations in a future situation, simply 'click' into this file to feel the same way again. For example, you could recall the calm and serenity from gazing across the ocean on your last big holiday when encountering a difficult employee, colleague or family member. Or you could recall the confidence and sense of accomplishment from finishing a big project when you're about to go into a job interview.

Bringing back the images, sensations, memories, and emotions associated with a flow experience can be extremely uplifting, exciting, and empowering; especially when revisited regularly.

Simple Boosts to Happiness

Now that you have the tools to challenge your feelings of frustration head-on, understand why playing is vital to life as a mum and have a flow-like experience to 'click' into for future boosts to happiness and confidence, here are a variety of scientifically-proven strategies to help increase your overall happiness on a regular basis to complete the journey:

- reflect at the end of each day and write down 3 things that went well and why they went well
- mentally take away a positive event in your life and contemplate what your life would be like without one of the good things in your life, e.g., your health, a good relationship, a safe neighbourhood, or a particular achievement

- choose one of your top character strengths (identified in Chapter One) and use it in a new way each day for one week — revisit the VIA Character website for tips on how you can use each of the 24 character strengths and choose one that suits you
- write a letter of gratitude to someone you have not previously thanked and, if appropriate, either meet the person and read the letter or mail it
- write about a moment in your life when a negative event led to unforeseen positive consequences
- practice mindfulness (see Chapter Three)
- write down a goal you want to reach and 2 specific steps you can do this week to make progress on your goal
- before you to go bed at night, close your eyes and imagine at least four positive events that could possibly happen the next day
- at the end of the day, write down 3 funny things that happened to you that day and why these things occurred
- identify a friend or stranger in need and spend a small amount of time or money on them
- track the acts of kindness you perform each day so that you can report the total by the end of the week
- take notice when someone does something deliberately kind for you and pay the kindness forward by being kind to 3 people that day

- go for a run or swim, or join in on a group fitness class
- play with a puppy or kitten (borrow one if you have to!)

Remember, this list is not exhaustive and not every strategy works for every person, but it is very likely that if you give each one a try, you'll find some easy sources of happiness for your life.

♥ ♥ ♥

The science of happiness is an ever-growing area of research that has had some significant findings and breakthroughs in the last decade, and there is some inspiring news that has come from this. Firstly, you have a lot of control over how happy you are and want to be, despite the physical, emotional and social challenges that come with being a busy mum.

Secondly, to live a happy journey through motherhood requires relatively simple, low-effort changes to your lifestyle. The key is to identify the need for change, make it and stick with it until it becomes a habit, and part of the journey. An advantage you have is that we now know it takes 5% less time to learn and create a new habit that involves 'play' than without. Now that's something to be happy about!

♥ ♥ ♥

Three actions you can now take:

1. Practice catching yourself during times of frustration and asking the four reflective questions.

2. Revisit and practice the flow creation exercise to cement the memory of sensations experienced for easier recall.

3. Choose one or two simple boosts to happiness from the list provided and try to implement them into your daily routine.

NIKKI COX

7

Strengthen Your Bonds

For many mums, feelings of loneliness and isolation as part of the motherhood journey come as a complete surprise. During the early stages, there is so much focus on the birth and the first month or two after you bring bub home that little thought is given to the reality of what your life will look like once you are caring for your child 24/7.

With my first child, I started feeling very lonely probably about a month after I had her. I spent the first five days in the hospital, then my mum came and stayed for two weeks. After that, my husband went back to working and I was completely on my own. I'd start planning things to fill up my days; appointments, errands, baby classes, playgroups, walks in the pram… but some days, aside from a phone call or two, I wouldn't talk to anyone for hours. I found the feelings of isolation and loneliness would quickly start washing over me and the tears would flow; mourning the social life and freedom I once had, the friendships that I had somehow 'lost' and the connections with my family living interstate, which I hadn't missed terribly much until then.

My early experiences with being a mum are unsurprisingly common, with various studies showing that more than 90 percent of mums admit to feeling lonely after having their first child. Although prevalent, many first-time mothers keep their experience of loneliness to themselves; trying to hide their feelings from partners and other people in their life. Something I can certainly relate to. And the loneliness and isolation you feel as a mum doesn't necessarily go away as your kids grow up.

As a busy mum with a busy life, you can often unintentionally invest less in your relationships with those around you as you focus on nurturing your children. This tends to happen much more with friends that either don't have kids or have kids that are significantly older than yours. You may feel like you don't have anything in common anymore, or that having to arrange catch-ups around your kids is too hard or burdensome for your friends.

Even if you're a working mum, surrounded by co-workers every day, you can feel extremely lonely. As a working mum, you tend to want to be more productive so that you can leave work on time and get home to your kids. This reduces the time to chat about office happenings, which can also make you feel out of the loop. Even if you were to strike up a conversation with someone at work, outside interests and activities of your childless co-workers are likely to be very different from your own.

But the greatest influence on your ability as a mum to re-establish old relationships and create new ones is to overcome the fear of being judged as a parent. Being a mum is a tough gig, but it's vital for you to remember that there is a great deal that unites us in this journey through motherhood.

Being connected to others socially is widely considered by experts of psychology, neuroscience, and sociology as a fundamental human need. It is crucial to both wellbeing and survival. Extreme examples have shown that babies who lack human contact fail to thrive and often die, and we have a long history of solitary confinement being used as a form of punishment. So it's unsurprising that, as a mum, connecting with people and maintaining strong, positive friendships is essential to living a happier life. The old adage 'it takes a village to raise a child' holds an enormous amount of truth; you can't go through motherhood alone.

Loneliness and isolation experienced by mums are usually felt across four key areas:

1. Work: if you were working before you had kids, and are yet to return to the workforce, you miss the daily contact with workmates (or just adults in general)

2. Social: you feel like you have to put your friendships (particularly with those who are childless) on the backburner while your kids are young, and then don't feel as though you can pick up where you left off

3. Financial: you may have found yourself, possibly for the first time in your adult life, without an income and therefore relying on your partner to bring home a paycheck, which may lead to feelings of vulnerability

4. Geographical: it is quite common for family units to be quite spread out, due to work, family or retirement relocation choices, and you may have found yourself without local family support

My personal experience with loneliness has ebbed and flowed through each of these areas at different times during motherhood. As an extrovert, and a fiercely independent woman, it felt like I was living someone else's life; unfamiliar thoughts and emotions around being utterly alone in my world with my kids were flooding my mind and I had no idea what to do about it. For quite some time I felt like I had no control over being lonely, and assumed that this was just a part of being a mother and raising children.

By the time both my children were 3 months old, I felt like I was going to explode. I wanted to share my day with someone who understood what I was going through; someone who cared about the little milestones, the struggles, the emotional rollercoaster and the moments of joy. I wanted to hear about the experiences of others to make me feel 'normal'.

When my kids were 6 months old, I was desperate for regular connection with other adults in the working world. I wanted to have conversations that were intellectually stimulating and get a little of my independence back.

Once my kids were a year old, I started to crave the deep, meaningful friendships I had somehow lost to motherhood, including with my husband and siblings. It felt like the previous 12 months were a blur; like I had been living in a bubble with my children, and the people I wase once close to had evolved, changed and grown without me. And I continue to experience these 'bubbles' from time-to-time.

Most mums want more mum friends. Whether you are a new mum, a mum with kids at school, a working mum, or a SAHM, the best place to start is to *slow down* your busy life.

This chapter will outline strategies I have used to tackle the feelings of loneliness and isolation that come with being a mum. It will encourage you to start slowly reaching out of your comfort zone to strengthen existing relationships, re-ignite old connections and create new ones.

Strengthening Existing Relationships

Strengthening bonds with your partner, family members and friends not only helps your relationships grow, but it can also provide some added benefits to your wellbeing.

Here are 5 small actions that are proven to contribute to the strengthening of an existing relationship, and don't take much time. Whilst my husband, my kids and I practice these actions regularly together, I find it's easy to forget to apply them to my other close relationships as well, which is just as important.

1. Kiss

Of course you enjoy a nice smooch with your partner, but when was the last time you properly kissed one another?

Kissing is a wonderful way to connect with each other, or even start something more.

Kissing can also reduce blood pressure, help prevent cavities by getting your saliva flowing, as well as giving you a mini facelift by working your facial muscles, especially through deep kissing. Kissing also increases your self-esteem by making you feel loved.

Aim to give your partner a good snog every day to reinforce your feelings for one another.

2. Hug longer than 20 seconds

Hugging comes more naturally to some people, can be culturally dependent and is appropriate for certain types of relationships more than others, but it gives us many benefits.

A whole-hearted embrace gives a sense of security and reduces stress. This reduction in stress helps our physical health and mental wellbeing. This is why our kids always feel better after a hug when they've had a fall or are upset.

Hugging stimulates the release of several neurotransmitters in our brains; dopamine, serotonin, and oxytocin. Dopamine is a pleasure hormone that gives us a good feeling, serotonin reduces pain and increases feelings of happiness, and oxytocin helps us feel trust and a sense of safety.

Look for opportunities to give someone a big warm hug… or start asking for them.

3. Cuddle

Unlike hugging, cuddling is not defined by arms and bodies connecting in a specific way. Cuddling could be anything from touching foreheads together, leaning against each other, or sitting side by side with an arm around someone.

Cuddling can be very powerful emotionally, socially, physically and mentally; so much so that there are even 'cuddle clubs' popping up around the world to facilitate hugs for those deeply in need of human connection!

4. Listen

You have two ears and only one mouth, so you should listen twice as much as you speak, but people rarely do. More often, when someone is speaking, we are only waiting for our turn to speak, rather than truly listening to what they have to say.

Listening is more than just hearing the words that someone says. When you listen, try to understand the person talking. When they have finished speaking, ask yourself 'What was the meaning that they were trying to get across? What were they feeling as they spoke? What is important to them?' Then ask any questions that you need to that will help clarify their meaning.

5. Say 'I Love You'

How often you tell a loved one that you love them doesn't equate to how much you love them, but doing it more will strengthen your bond. Expressing your love out loud is a way of confirming that you care.

More often, as a mum, you typically demonstrate your love through your actions, like preparing meals with love. Actions do speak louder than words but don't forget that words have tremendous power also.

Get Your Giggle On

One of the best feelings in the world is a good, authentic laugh. It can bring people together and establish amazing connections. Everything from a little giggle to a side-splitting cackle can change the mood of a room. Some days it's hard *not* to laugh when you have kids!

There is so much to love about laughter; firstly, it can lead to a longer life as a result of:
- enhanced moods
- decreases in blood pressure
- decreases in stress-related hormones
- reduced levels of anxiety and depression
- decreased hunger hormones

- lower cholesterol levels
- overall increased immunity

In addition, laughing can tone your abs, give you a low impact cardio workout and can help ease physical pain.

Secondly, you are 30 times more likely to laugh at something when you are with other people than when you are alone. Sharing a laugh with someone you are already close to can:

- encourage attraction
- strengthen the relationship
- create memories that improve relationship satisfaction when remembered

So, how can you get your giggle on more? You don't need to perform a comedy routine, but if you already know how to make someone laugh, see if you can increase how often you do it. In addition, here are 10 quick ways to share laughter with those around you:

1. Find the humour in daily situations and share it with a friend or family member
2. Watch your favourite stand-up comedian on YouTube/Netflix together
3. Listen to a funny podcast together
4. Go out with friends for a karaoke night

5. Re-watch a comedy sitcom or movie that always cracks you both up
6. Play with a dog together (even if you have to borrow one from a friend)
7. Look through old photos together
8. Find humour in your most embarrassing moments and share the story with a close friend
9. Read through the humour cards in a gift shop together
10. Just watch your kids together!

Re-Ignite Old Connections

When I became pregnant, I had no idea that some of my friends had some very specific ideas about how I should raise and parent my child. It was only after I started making choices about what sort of mum I wanted to be that these friends decided to voice their opinions; even argue with me about it and, eventually, chose to remove me from their lives.

I also had friends that I simply couldn't see as often as I used to after having kids, and our friendships faded into the past. Life simply took us in separate directions and trying to keep the friendship going became too difficult. In most cases there were no negative feelings shared over the situation; we just silently agreed that continuing the friendship no longer made sense.

I know I'm not the only mum who has lost friends to motherhood, but the experience can be confusing, disappointing, hurtful and disparaging; it is also, sometimes, completely unavoidable.

But it's important to understand that friendships don't always last forever, and at the risk of sounding cliché, people will come in and out of your life at all stages, for one reason or another. In any case, the friendships you have are important whilst they exist, but how long a friendship lasts does not change how important they are.

True friendships are with those that love you for who you are but also remind you of who you are or who you could become (your skills, talents, qualities, and passions). Whilst it is easy to neglect these precious friendships when motherhood ensues — particularly with those who may not be mothers themselves — good friends will:

- see you through many of life's ups and downs, even when you have been out of touch for a while
- make time for each other, even if it's just a quick phone call
- don't forget anniversaries, birthdays or other dates that are important to *you*
- always be honest

- look out for each other's wellbeing, e.g. when you've had too many drinks
- support one another's endeavours, even if you don't completely see eye-to-eye

Even if your friend doesn't have children, you should be able to talk to them about yours. Don't overdo it, of course, but occasionally sharing things about your children makes a personal connection. If an occasion happens that you need to cancel a catch-up to attend to a sick child, a friend who may have seen a photo or heard a cute story about your child will naturally be more understanding and caring.

So simply reach out to an old friend; a text message, an email, a Facebook message or a phone call. A good friend will take steps to re-ignite the connection you once had and work with you to re-build it. Everyone else probably isn't worth your precious time and energy.

Creating New Bonds

There is an endless number of ways that people, in general, meet new friends. The first step to making new friends as a mum, however, is to move past fears connected with being judged and having to be a 'perfect parent'.

Take a look at some of the most popular mum-related videos and blog posts online. The vast majority of these highlight parenting 'fails' or imperfections. Mums love seeing or reading about other mum's failing or struggling; not because we enjoy gloating about *not* failing, but because it reminds us that other mums struggle as much as we do. Mums like me are going through the same fears, worries, and joys as mums like you (otherwise you probably wouldn't be reading this book!).

We may all differ in some way; make different decisions, have different interests, have different daily routines, have different priorities, but reaching out to make new mum friends shouldn't feel as scary as it does. It's all about finding what connects you to someone else.

Here are a few ways to find new friends as a mum:

1. If you work, make a new connection with another mum by asking about their kids, sharing a story about your kids, or simply talking about the trials and tribulations of parenting

2. If your kids are young, join a parents group or baby class and chat about age-related challenges, then arrange to meet up again for a coffee date

3. Smile at every mum you meet; it may be the only smile she gets all day and could lead to a conversation

4. Visit a local park or play centre and start a conversation with a mum there on her own about your children, then arrange for future playdates at the same location

5. If your children are older, strike up a conversation with a mum on her own also attending an extra-curricular or sporting event, then swap phone numbers or connect on Facebook

6. Sign up for the free Mush app (a bit like Tinder for mums!), create your profile and scroll through other profiles to connect with like-minded, local mums in your area

7. Find a reason to leave the house and talk to people that you may have something in common with; a new class that interests you, or join a group of like-minded people

The key is to get out there and start talking to people *without* the intention to make new friends but to simply *connect*. Friendships will grow from a continuous connection over time, with the people you feel most comfortable with.

The saying is true; it really does take a village to raise a child. But Australian parents are moving homes, jobs, and countries at a faster rate than ever before. This makes it increasingly

difficult for you, as a mum, to create a network of mutual support. It is important to remind yourself of the importance of establishing and maintaining strong, personal connections during motherhood. Without the help of partners, family, and friends, both new and old, you have less opportunity to feel socially connected during a time of potential loneliness and isolation.

Taking simple steps to ensure you have strong relationships in your life will unlock the resources needed to make your life easier as you navigate the hurdles of parenthood. That, in turn, relieves stress and allows you to look at being a mother with more optimism and happiness.

Three actions you can now take:
1. Practice the 5 small actions (kiss, hug, cuddle, listen and say 'I love you') with those closest to you every day.
2. Create opportunities for more laughter in your life, then start sharing these experiences with various other people.
3. Start stepping out of your comfort zone by choosing one or two ways for creating a new connection from the list provided and try them out.

8

Love What You Do

Whether you have returned to work already, or are planning on it, going back to work after full-time parenting can be daunting; even when you have a job you love.

You will likely feel a huge mix of emotions; the excitement of working and spending time with adults again, the anxiety about your child's care (if they are younger), the guilt associated with doing something for yourself, the pain of going back to work earlier than you want, the stress of juggling the workloads both in your job and in your home… and some of these emotions don't ever seem to go away.

For me, returning to work was the catalyst for why I do what I do now. Before having my daughter I *loved* my job, and I had worked hard to get it. After my struggles with becoming a mum and shifting into this new, unpredictable, highly demanding (but ever-so rewarding) role, I soon craved connection with other adults, stimulation from adult conversations, a predictable and logical part to my daily routine and a space where I could be creative, challenged and use my skills and talents again.

But my head and heart felt torn; anguish doesn't come close to describe the experience of making the decision to return to work and put my daughter into childcare. I tried applying logic to the situation in every way I could; the socialisation skills she would gain, the physical and mental break I would get from full-time parenting, the relief from financial stress our family would receive, the happier mum I could become for my daughter by living a more fulfilled life… but when you are burdened so deep with doubt and anxiety, it can be extremely hard to make decisions like this with confidence.

I confided in my husband, other mums and a few health professionals, but in my heart-of-hearts, I knew the right decision was to return to work. And on the first day back, I cried the whole way there, during my lunch break and all the way home. But at least I loved what I did for work, right?

It's not long after you return to the working world that you quickly realise how much has changed in the time you've been away; no matter how long you've been gone. These changes, along with your self-doubt in the ability to actually do your job again to the same level as before, can very quickly lead to a dislike for your profession, your industry or even working in general. You can feel resentment towards your employers, maybe even your kids, and possibly regret for your decision.

I felt all of this, and no longer had the passion and love for my job, as I once did. Worst of all, I felt *stuck*.

♥ ♥ ♥

Many women suffer a crisis of confidence when they have been away from work for a long period of time, and worry a lot about their job performance. To add to this, if your children are little, you also start to worry about how they are coping without you. As a working mum, your emotional state is about as stable as a wonky donkey, but you have to give the impression that you've got-it-together, which just adds to your stress levels.

The key to handling the stress and overwhelming emotions that accompany the return to work as a mum is to find ways to love what you do, why you do it and who you are when you do it.

Contrary to popular belief, as a mum, you are allowed to be a *person*. I know it sounds silly, but sometimes we really do need reminding; you have dreams, desires, and passions. And being a 'whole person' for your kids; not just 'Mum', who apparently ceased to be an actual human being after giving birth, makes you a better parent to them.

You are allowed to love your job, and it doesn't mean you don't love your kids, or that you love work more than your kids. Research even shows that, whether or not a woman works in the first five years of her child's life has absolutely no bearing on their childhood development. Feeling guilt over doing what you love is not only insane but entirely misguided. You *need* to enjoy work, not only for yourself but so that you are setting an example for your kids to pursue what they love. Finding the right job for you can mean:

- no longer missing out on much-needed enthusiasm and energy that comes with finding your work highly meaningful and engaging
- allaying feelings of doubt and guilt from being at work, instead of with your kids
- your children will grow up learning that work doesn't have to be a place of resentment; instead, it can be somewhere to grow, inspire and achieve!

Do you look forward to going to work? Do you come home energised by what you've achieved during the day?

Going to a job where your gifts, talents, and skills are able to be applied in ways that are meaningful and fulfilling, and you are surrounded with positive, encouraging, and supportive co-workers is fundamental to being a happy working parent.

If you want to transition from 'working person' to a happy, satisfied 'working mum', regardless of whether you are already in the workforce, this chapter will guide you through ways to make it happen. You will discover tools to help you find a job that you can enjoy, start loving the job you are already in and create a balance between work, family and personal time.

Many of the strategies outlined in the next section may require some deeper thinking and reflection. It may be useful at this point to grab your journal or a pen and paper before you read on.

Looking For the Right Job

Regardless of whether you are currently working or not, let's start your search for a job you can enjoy whilst you're away from your little ones by answering a series of out-of-the-box, yet thought-provoking questions:

- What subject could you read 500 books about without getting bored?
- What could you do for five years straight without getting paid?
- What would you spend your time doing if you had complete financial abundance to do anything?
- What hobbies did you enjoy doing before life got in the way?
- Imagine that you are very old. What do you wish you had spent the last 20 to 30 years doing?
- What type of role would you be excited to tell your friends and family about?
- What projects (paid, volunteer or school-oriented) have you most enjoyed working on and why?

Don't worry if you can't answer all of these questions; it's not a test! The idea is to get you thinking about possibilities you had not considered before, or help you to reignite a passion that was already there for jobs you have perhaps held in the past.

Meet Pria

Pria was a mum of one looking to return to the workforce after four years. She had recently moved to Australia and wanted to find a job that she could pour her passion and love into.

Pria started her job-hunting journey by looking at her top character strengths, hobbies and interests. She had a love for connecting people, in particular families, and a keen interest in herbs.

After investigating the tea industry, Pria decided to start sourcing, creating and selling her own, boutique herbal tea blends and developed partnerships to create a place where friends and families could come to enjoy her creations and learn more about the art of tea brewing.

Now that you've had a bit of a think about what drives you, to help you further in working out what job might help you feel happy, energised and fulfilled, let's play a short game. The 'Career Interests Game' (which can be found at https://career.missouri.edu/career-interest-game/) has been designed to help you match your interests and skills with job types. It can help you begin thinking about how your identity will fit in with specific work environments.

The game is based on the theory by Dr. John Holland, psychologist and former Professor of Sociology at John Hopkins University, that people and work environments can be put into six different groups (Social, Enterprising,

Conventional, Realistic, Investigative and Artistic), and certain parts of peoples' identities may find particular environments more appealing. While you may align to several of the six groups, you may be attracted primarily to two or three.

To start the game, first, imagine walking into a room in which the six different groups of people are already interacting.

Next, go the website above, click on links for each group type at the top of the page, and read through the descriptions. Decide the group you would be drawn to first, then your second choice, and finally your third choice. Jot these down if you need to.

Most people and most jobs are a combination of two or three of these group types. Have a browse through the 'Career Possibilities' section under the group descriptions for your first, second and third choices on the website; these lists will give you a great indication of what jobs might suit you.

As an added bonus, the 'Hobbies' section under each group description can also help you choose a new hobby to try in your 'me' time, to inject more fun and happiness in your life.

So by now, you might have some idea of what sort of jobs may suit you, drive you, connect with you and make you happy. Don't worry too much about making a solid decision or the logistics that may be involved at this stage; this chapter is about getting you started on the path to loving work. Like anything, it's a process, which may be short, long, hard, easy or somewhere in between. The important thing is to start moving forward and maintain momentum. With that in mind, let's now look at some practical ways you can work towards getting into a job you'll love.

Firstly, you can volunteer. Volunteering is a great way to meet new people and expand your network beyond your existing circle of friends, colleagues, and acquaintances. You might end up finding a new opportunity you never thought about before, or meet someone who can give you a hand on the way to where you want to go.

Find a charity or a cause that means something to you and get involved. You'll meet more people who care about what you do and gain great new skills and experience at the same time.

Secondly, you can learn something new. New jobs that have never been heard of are being created every day. To stay relevant, it's important that you see yourself as a lifetime learner.

A great way to expand your job options, or break back into the workforce, is to explore further education and vocational training. By refreshing your skills, or retraining in a new field, you're increasing your chances of finding employment that plays to your strengths, adding to your profile of skills and more importantly, boosting your confidence!

Lastly, acknowledge your new skills. 'What new skills?' I hear you ask... well, you're a mum, and being a mum is one of the hardest jobs in the world; it's unpaid, often undervalued and sometimes taken completely for granted. But whilst there is no formal training for becoming a mum, there have been tonnes of on-the-job learning. Being at home with kids has actually taught me creativity, stress management, problem-solving, multi-tasking and time management like no other job I've ever had.

Find Love for the Job You Have

Sadly, most mums (and certainly, most people in general) say they work in a job they don't actually like and are not sure what to do about it, other than simply finding a new job. But perhaps it's not *what* you do, but how you *view* it and how you *do* it.

Currently termed 'Job Crafting', changing the way you view or describe what you do, and focusing on the aspects of the job you love the most, can reignite a passion for what you do.

For example, if you're an accountant, do you see yourself as a rule-abiding number cruncher, or are you actively helping people to understand their finances and make smart decisions for their families and businesses? If you're an admin assistant, do you see yourself as a paper-filing answering machine, or are you central to the smooth processing and efficiency of a department or organisation?

Likewise, sometimes the way to enjoy your job is to redesign what you currently do to better suit your identity and play to your strengths.

Keen for more people interaction in your role? Perhaps you could offer to provide training or mentoring to others. Being a mentor to someone younger in your workplace can boost your enthusiasm for what you do. Imparting your skills, knowledge, and talents could also positively impact your workplace as a whole.

Finding your job boring or unchallenging? Look for an opportunity to learn something new by raising your hand and signing up for a development program on offer at work, or take a short course on your own. Not only will it open your mind, but as soon as you start learning something new you will also get excited about work again.

Alternatively, an easy first step would be to rearrange your days to schedule the tasks that you do find enjoyable for times when you need a burst of energy, like first thing in the morning or right after lunch.

Make a list of all the things you like, or love, about your current job. *Why* do you love them? What would you miss if you couldn't work anymore, or were forced to work elsewhere?

Reminding yourself of the parts of your job that you find rewarding, stimulating and enjoyable can be a real buzz, and can even make you feel like you're getting some of your former identity back. Job crafting is all about ditching that 'grin and bear it' strategy, and focusing on what you do best, what you like the most and working as though what you do matters — because it does!

Otherwise, if you find that job crafting isn't giving you that spark you need to start loving what you do, maybe it's time to think about whether your current position is still a good fit. The average person changes careers multiple times in their life, so you may need to consider this for yourself. Perhaps think about why you got into your field of work originally, and whether you're still on the same path.

The Illusive Work-Life Balance

One of the most common discussions amongst working parents concerns the concept of 'work-life balance'. We all have limited time, and naturally, it makes sense that you don't want to over-commit to any one area or sacrifice one for the other.

While the idea of having balance is important, such discussions are often misguided. Work-life balance strategies often separate your life from work and put them into competition with each other, but the real goal should be work-life *integration*.

If you think about how much time the average person spends working (approximately 80,000 hours, or 9 full years, by some estimates), it becomes clear that there isn't really a way to separate work from life. The daily actions you take as a part of your job become ingrained in you as habits, which shapes parts of your identity (as discussed in Chapter One). While having some boundaries in place is important, work-life integration (and ultimately enjoying what you do for work) is about aligning who you are as a result of work into a larger, holistic way of operating as a person, and a mum.

Look at it this way; if you're an artist, you are an artist outside of your studio. You probably take a creative approach to menial tasks such as cooking dinner, arranging furniture in the house or gardening. You would also tend to do more creativity-based activities with your kids.

If you're a nurse, you are likely to be a nurse after your shift ends. You probably react very quickly and calmly to situations as they pop up at home, and instinctively focus on what's happening right now in your family life, rather than what might occur a few years down the track.

What skills and talents do you use at work that you also use in other areas of life?

Work-life integration is blending together these two areas of your life in a way that works towards a greater quality of life. It's not about the amount of time you give to one area compared to the other, but rather the equilibrium you create so that both areas are supporting you in living a happy, fulfilling life. What this looks like, however, will be different for every mum.

To figure out the right working pattern for you, you may have to think outside of the box. Flexible working for a parent does not just mean working part-time hours; it can be so much more than that. For example:

- compress your hours so you can do five days' worth of work in four
- delay your start or finish times to allow you to pick up or drop off your children from school during term times
- consider doing project work only, so you work full-time hours for a project and then take time off in lieu
- work some of your hours from home
- enquire about job share arrangements

The reality is there is no single formula for mixing work and family. I have met and known so many mums over the years, and all of them have designed their work-life integration differently. Some have remained out of the workforce for five years or so when their kids were small, and now love working in a full-time role. Some didn't work for decades, but now have successful careers in the latter part of their life. And some have managed to work through the years when their kids were younger and only stepped back once they became teenagers.

The key is to regularly evaluate your circumstances (needs, wants, emotions) and take steps towards changing the things you need to change. This might mean a conversation with your partner, your childcare provider, your boss or the HR manager; or it could mean creating a more solid schedule to ensure you are making time for work, relationships, family and, of course, yourself.

Just remember that any work arrangement you establish doesn't have to be permanent. Remind yourself that if your childcare situation isn't working for you, you can change it. If the schedule you set for yourself isn't working, you can discuss it with your manager. And if your job just isn't sustainable for your family in the long run, start looking for a more family-friendly option. Change isn't easy, but it is always possible.

♥ ♥ ♥

Work is a part of life for most mums, so you need to find a way to enjoy it, rather than resent it or view it as a necessary 'evil'. Over and above a source of finance, it's a chance for you to grow, learn, be inspired, inspire others, excel, connect and contribute to the world.

Fundamentally, work is a large part of life and needs to be invested in to live a happy, satisfying existence.

♥ ♥ ♥

Three actions you can now take:

1. If you are looking for a job to love, reflect on your answers to the out-of-the-box questions outlined earlier in this chapter and discuss them with a close friend or family member for some further insight.

2. If you are looking to find love in the job you already have, first write down a warm way of describing what you actually do. Post this description somewhere you can read it whilst you work and start thinking of ways you can enhance the work experience (new skills, responsibilities, tasks) to better suit the aspects of your job you love the most.

3. Reflect on your current work-life integration (or start planning what you want it to look like when you return to work) — Where does it feel out of balance? What steps can you take to start making changes towards creating equilibrium between the different parts of your life in order for you to feel happier?

NIKKI COX

9

Energy Synergy

Motherhood is profoundly fulfilling, but it is also the most physically, emotionally and mentally demanding activity anyone could ever do; and it gets done day after day, 24/7 for many, many years. The job certainly gets harder the more kids you have, or if any of your children have special needs.

There is no doubt that some dads are great; fantastic with the kids, committed to mutual parenting, do their fair share around the house and are overall very supportive. But this isn't always the case. If you add up both paid and unpaid work, the average mum works significantly more than her partner.

And if you're a single mum, as one in five mothers in Australia are, you're getting little to no help from a partner at all.

Then, in the back of your mind your mum-brain is constantly on the go; to-do lists that never seem to end and always trying to remember one thing or another, forever distracting you and invading your ability to truly relax or take a breath.

To add to all of this is the constant anxiety, or worry, that comes with motherhood. Termed 'hyper-vigilance', it's basically being in a heightened state of sensory sensitivity, where you are constantly in protection mode on behalf of your children, who are too young to do it for themselves properly, if at all. Thanks to maternal biological changes we go through during pregnancy, we even sleep in this state!

No wonder mums constantly feel drained and depleted.

Whenever you've been asked by a friend, partner or family member how you are doing, how often have you answered with "Tired"? Sure, sometimes you do feel tired, but sometimes there is something more going on than sleep deprivation; something deeper.

Before having kids, I had a lot of energy and felt fit and healthy. If I wanted to stay up late or go out for a night on the town, there was no question about my ability to stay alert and engaged. I could spontaneously go on trips or to events without even needing to worry about my physical capacity to maintain the energy required to enjoy myself. But now, with two kids, I'm more easily run down, I can get colds frequently, and my menstrual cycle can have a mind of its own.

But I'm a mum, so it's normal to feel tired and lack energy all the time, right? Not at all!

Having energy is essential to living well and getting the most out of life, but sometimes you can feel depleted for a myriad of reasons, and it's *not* just because of your kids. Even if you are lucky enough to regularly eat well and get enough sleep, you can still feel a distinct lack of energy and zest for life.

♥ ♥ ♥

As mums, we have enough to stress about without adding to it unnecessarily. While stress is fundamental to our survival, it is also possibly the most dangerous toxin your body faces every day. It can deplete you of the energy needed to live well and get the most out of life. Stress-reduction techniques have been scattered throughout the previous chapters of this book (e.g. mind-body approaches, mindfulness practices, investing in self-care and 'me' time, strengthening relationships), however controlling some of the causes of your stress can also help you cope with the uncontrollable.

Unfortunately, many of us care too much about things that simply don't matter, and ignore things we actually *should* focus on. Women, in general, tend to overthink things so much that it can become an obsession. Then, all of sudden, life has become a constant wave of stress, instead of being full of fun and happiness. I know I have worried about whether my kids have had too much screen time, not enough tummy time, if they've gone to bed at the 'right' time, or if they've had balanced diet across the day (and sometimes still do!). But really, that stuff doesn't matter in the grand scheme of things. So you let your 6-year-old have an ice-cream, some hot chips, and a juice bottle today? Look at the wider picture — they probably had a decent serving of fruit, vegetables, whole grains, and dairy most days this week, and were happy to be spoilt by Mum today.

Imagine your stress and worry is like a glass of water. If you hold onto the glass for a minute or so, it probably won't be a problem. If you hold onto it for an hour, you're likely to start getting an ache in your arm. But if you hold onto it for a day, or longer, your arm is going to feel numb and paralysed.

If your stress and worry is beginning to hurt you or, worse still, make you feel paralysed and incapable of doing anything, you need to remember to put the glass down! Stop and evaluate what is causing you stress and ask yourself — do I really *need* to be worrying about this? What is the worst that can happen?

At what point are you going to decide to stop stressing about things that don't matter, and start caring about the things that do?

Stress, worry, and anxiety are the biggest drains on your energy levels as a mum. Reading this chapter will help you to discover the most common things mums stress about *needlessly*, in order to help you evaluate your own sources of stress.

A disorganised, clutter-filled home is not only a symptom of stress but can also be another unnecessary source of stress, according to researchers at the University of California, Los Angeles (UCLA) who explored the relationship between 32 families and the objects in their homes. It turns out that clutter has a profound effect on your mood, self-esteem and, subsequently, your energy levels.

This is not to say that your home must always be clean and tidy (a near impossibility when you have children around!), however, your home can easily become filled to the brim with 'things' you don't really need or want. Without even noticing it, we surround ourselves with unnecessary, energy-draining clutter; clutter which creates a negative environment for those living within it.

According to neuroscientists, clutter bombards our minds with excessive stimuli (visual, tactile, etc.), which causes our senses to work overtime on stimuli that aren't necessary or important. This triggers the release of the stress hormone cortisol, which increases tension and anxiety, and can start impacting your immune system, heart, lungs, and other key physiological functions.

From a mental health perspective, when you're surrounded by more things than you can manage, it sends a message that your life is out of control. It can then cause a cascade of negative emotions, for example when looking at a messy closet, you can feel *stressed* at the lack of organisation, *guilty* that you don't wear half of what you own, and *confused* as to what kind of style you're even going for.

Decluttering your house by throwing away old things can give you mental clarity, focus, peace, and balance. You will be able to concentrate for longer periods of time because your brain is not trying to process the added stimuli.

Getting rid of clutter can also help you let go of the past, including those unhelpful sources of stress and worry, and give you a renewed sense of freedom and control over your life. It generates fresh energy and can inspire you to start making positive changes in your life.

And looking at decluttering in a practical sense, less stuff means less to take care of, which means more time to spend elsewhere, such as with your kids!

So, in addition to throwing a magnifying glass over your sources of stress, this chapter is also going to provide tips for decluttering, as well as walk you through identifying what other things might be draining energy from you, and how to plug the energy leaks in your life.

Unnecessary Stress

Here are the top 7 things that women, in general, worry about or stress over that are absolutely *not* worth your energy:

1. What Other People Think Of You

Worrying about what others think of you stems from the fear that you may be left without friends or intimacy. One way to break this cycle is to consistently live your life from a place of *other-centeredness*, rather than self-centeredness. If you are consistently kind and considerate, then you will spend less energy worrying about what others think of you.

2. How Much Money You Have

Research has shown us over and over again that more money does not equate to more happiness. Studies have shown that money makes a difference when it means living in a home versus having to live on the streets, but beyond your basic needs, having more money won't make you happier. Practicing gratitude for what you already have (covered in more detail in Chapter Ten) is the perfect way to overcome this way of thinking, and the stress it can cause.

3. Your Past Mistakes

Everyone makes mistakes in life; big and small. At some point, you have to just forgive yourself for the past and move on. Dwelling on past experiences will not change them or make you feel any better about where you are now. Remember that every mistake allows you to grow and learn, so look at your mistakes as blessings in disguise. Start embracing the mistakes you have made in the past as vital life experiences that helped you get to where you are now.

4. Fitting In

Meeting the status quo and finding your place in this world has been drilled into most of us for so long now that we've almost started to believe that fitting in is vital to a happy life. Going along with the crowd, however, almost never results in true happiness. By trying to fit in with certain groups, you're sacrificing the beautiful things that make you unique. But why would you want to change who you are as a person for other people? Following your heart and your true passions are far more likely to lead you down a better road.

5. Looking Perfect

The perfect body doesn't exist, so stop wasting energy on trying to mould yours into what society tells you it must look like. We all have unique physical appearances, and while you can always try to improve your physical fitness, this should have more to do with your health, rather than your looks. Try taking a break from the mirror, or smiling more. As clichéd as it sounds, people like other people who smile, regardless of their physical features.

6. Being Perfect

This is one of my biggest struggles. It took me years to learn (even before kids, but more so after) how to be ok with letting perfection slide. In some areas of my life, I have managed to let go more than others, so I am, myself, a work-in-progress. I can tell you, however, that with these life-learnings a great deal of weight has been lifted and energy restored in my day.

So let me tell you now: it is *ok* to leave the breakfast dishes in their place until you get home from a day out of school drop-off and pick-ups, playgroup and grocery shopping. It is *ok* to fall asleep with your kids and catch up on some much-needed sleep, instead of cleaning a messy kitchen. If you're like me and love a clean slate every morning, you won't love it, but it won't mean that everything else must be put on hold until you tidy up. Let it go, it'll get done, life will go on; you can still have a great day. Let go of trying to be a perfect person / parent / homemaker, and focus your energy on being grateful for and enjoying your life with your family.

7. Pleasing Others

People-pleasing might win you some friends, but it won't win you any good ones. When you bend over backward to please others, you will inevitably attract the wrong kinds of people who just want to take advantage of you. Learning how to listen to your own needs, and say 'no' when you need to will not only help to keep balanced friendships that are based on more than you trying to please them, but will help you choose who are the people in your life you really *want* to please.

How to Declutter

Fortunately, unlike other more commonly recognised sources of stress, clutter is one of the easiest life stressors to fix. More and more women are starting to get on-board with reducing clutter, particularly with the rise in popularity of the show 'Tidying Up with Marie Kondo'. Cleaning stuff out can be a hard task, however, especially if you haven't done it for a while, but you will probably be surprised how many useless things you are holding on to and stressing yourself out with.

You may not be able to throw out, re-purpose, sell, donate, give away or recycle many things at the same time, so instead of setting aside a huge chunk of time to declutter, make it into a little challenge for yourself. This way, decluttering won't seem like such a monumental task to fit into your busy mum-life.

Here are 7 simple steps to get going with decluttering:

1. Start small, even if it's only with a single drawer or cupboard. Starting with the bedroom is ideal, as it can help create a relaxing space you may need!

2. Make decluttering a quick 15-minute weekly routine, and schedule it in.

3. Get in the habit of putting things away where they belong, rather than 'doing it later', and ask the members of your household to do the same.

4. Store away rarely used items, and dispose or donate unused ones.

5. Use plenty of containers when storing items.

6. Have friends help, as they aren't as attached to your things as you are.

7. Teach your kids to be responsible for their mess, and follow your 'decluttering lead'.

I have always been a minimalist myself; I routinely go through my wardrobe each season and donate any unused items from the previous season to charity. Each December I go through my kids' toys and find those that are unused or have no sentimental value, then have my kids come along to donate them to a local Christmas toy drive. I regularly donate 'play' clothes that no longer fit my kids to local childcare centres to use as spares. And any charity call-outs for unwanted items prompt me to put effort into searching my house for anything I can give that they are in need of; which isn't always possible, of course. These are great triggers throughout the year for regular, habitual decluttering in my home.

Understanding Energy Leaks

Now that you have identified possible sources of stress and worry that are siphoning your energy, the next step is to get a better understanding of the concept of energy to identify what can energise you, and what depletes you.

Energy, in the realm of wellness, comes in four main forms: Physical, Emotional, Mental and Spiritual. Regularly examining each type of energy can help you make lifestyle changes that can have a positive effect on your energy levels.

Physical Energy

- Are you eating a balanced diet and taking supplements where needed?
- Do you take your time eating (where you can) in an unstressed state?
- What are your sleep patterns like? Are you getting good quality sleep, when you do get it?
- Do you take the time to breathe deeply regularly? If you are seated often at home/work/in the car, does your position restrict your ability to breathe properly?
- Are you well hydrated?
- How often do you move and exercise? What sort of exercise do you do? Do you feel fit?

Emotional Energy

- Do you have strong and regular connections with friends, work colleagues and family?
- Do you stop to acknowledge, express and explore emotions as they are felt?
- What is the balance between your work and play? Does it suit your lifestyle?

- Are you able to easily find fun in your life? How often do you have a good laugh?
- Do you acknowledge, feel and express gratitude regularly?
- How often do you perform acts of kindness towards yourself and others?

Mental Energy

- Are you mentally challenged and stimulated enough?
- How often are you rewarded and/or acknowledged?
- If you work, is your work environment uplifting?
- What is your self-talk like — positive or negative?
- How regularly do you apply mindfulness techniques in your everyday life?
- When was the last time you had a meaningful, truthful, two-way conversation with someone?

Spiritual Energy

- Are you aware of your changed values after children?
- Are you connected with those values and make each decision with them in mind? (e.g. If you value hard work, and your day to day requires little effort, then your overall energy will still be affected)
- How often do you connect with nature? How immersed do you become when you do this?

- Do you regularly tune in and listen to your instincts?
- What are your dreams? Are you progressing towards them?

It's easy for mums to link their depleted energy levels to lack of sleep and stress, but as you can see, energy can leak from so many different places in our lives. Most of these energy leakage points are covered in detail throughout the chapters in this book. Once you understand where *your* energy may be leaking' from, identifying what changes you may need to make in your life to rebuild your energy levels becomes easier.

♥ ♥ ♥

You will always have moments in life where you feel extra stressed, and sometimes you won't even realise how burnt out and drained of energy you actually are. But it is unrealistic to expect to always feel like Supermum; able to manage everything that motherhood throws at you, on your own.

Taking the time to stop and reflect on what is happening around and inside of you causing you to stress is the most important thing you can do to regain energy and a sense of control over life. Through this heightened awareness, you can start taking the necessary steps towards changing your thoughts, beliefs, habits or routines to reduce your daily stressors and plug the energy leaks in your life.

Learning to manage your energy effectively can make a tremendous difference in your overall mood, concentration levels, patience, thoughts, and feelings.

♥ ♥ ♥

Three actions you can now take:
1. Identify which of the top 7 things women unnecessarily stress about relates to you, and choose one of these to actively start letting go of.

2. Choose one drawer or cupboard to declutter, and schedule in 15 minutes during your week to work through it.

3. Reflect on the four energy types and identify which of these has the biggest amount of 'leakage' for you. Choose one of the 'leaks' within that energy type and plan steps this week to plug that leak.

10

Bedtime Blessings

Were you told, before you became a mum, how tired you would feel day-to-day?

Did you believe it?

Tiredness is a regular state of being as soon as you become a mum. No one tells you about how the overwhelming tiredness as a parent would soak into your bones. You become highly irritable, your body and mind become slower and you desperately seek solitude, away from the noise of loud children.

Before I became a mum, I knew that pulling an 'all-nighter' to go dancing with friends, talk on the phone late into the night or study for an exam was manageable. Being tired wasn't such a bad thing when I knew that over the next night or two I could just catch up on sleep. But once you become a parent, there's no more staying up to 2 am every night and sleeping in til 10 or 11 — that life is gone. Now, once the birds start singing, it's pretty much wake-up time, and there's almost no opportunity to catch-up on lost or poor sleep.

If you're anything like me, you're a mum that sometimes just wants to lay about and not *do* much in the morning… but there is parenting to be done. As a mum, you find ways to work with tiredness, because when you have your kids around, you are 'on duty'.

It's easy to believe that other mothers 'handle it all perfectly', and then feel down about the fact that you either struggle yourself to get out of bed in the morning or make it past 3 pm with your eyes still open, but you really can't judge a book by its cover. Most mothers go through bouts of excessive tiredness where they are just plain worn out, both physically and mentally.

There never seems to be enough hours in a day to get things done, and somewhere you have to fit some sleep in there as well. The tiredness constantly lingers, and some days it can be hard to handle, but there *are* ways to cope.

Every mum knows that having kids means losing sleep. The sleep deprivation journey begins before you even give birth, during your months of pregnancy. Next, it's the long nights waking to feed and change your newborn, then you face teething, colds and coughs, nightmares, early morning wake-ups… and just when you think you might be able to start catching up on all that lost sleep, you're staying up late waiting for your teenagers to sneak in the back door, just to know they are safe.

A key problem contributing to our sleep issues as mothers, according to Dr. Thomas Roth (former president of the Sleep Research Society, and founding president of the National Sleep Foundation), is that as a culture, we tend to look down on sleep. Getting too much, or even just enough, can make us look like we are 'soft', with some sleep-deprived mums even taking pride in doing too much and sleeping too little; trading war stories of sleepless nights with other mums for sympathy and recognition. But a critical part in your battle against tiredness as a mum is to change your attitude about sleep.

Sleep is just as important to good health as diet, exercise, and connection with other people; and it needs to be seen this way. Not sleeping well can contribute to obesity, mental health issues, stress, type 2 diabetes, cardiovascular disease… honestly, if you pick a disease or health problem at random from a medical journal, it's probably worsened by or linked to poor sleep. But if looking after your own health isn't enough to get you to change your view on sleep, remember that you're not the only one affected by your sleep habits. If you're constantly tired, your whole family will feel it.

There are, of course, many other reasons why mothers are tired all the time; well beyond being woken during the night by their children. In previous chapters, you have uncovered many of the contributing factors to the tiredness, burnout, and fatigue felt by mums, including mental load, overwhelming guilt, unrealistic expectations of yourself to be Supermum, lack of replenishment through self-care and 'me' time, and energy 'leaks'. Making small, positive changes to handle these exhausting parts of life as a mum is essential to feeling less tired, but so too is changing the way you treat sleep. I know that there are 101 things to do or enjoy after the kids go to sleep… and whilst self-care during this time is important, so too is sleep. Finding a balance is key.

So, your sleep disruption and constant tiredness boil down to one thing: you're a mother. But is there anything you can do about it?

I firmly believe that you should never tell a mum to 'get more sleep'. We *know* we need more sleep; we feel it in every fibre of our being, and I'm pretty damn sure we would get more if we could! So this chapter *won't* be doing that. Instead, I'm going to give you some tips on how to cope with tiredness during your busy life as a mum, and how to make the most of the sleep you *can* get, so that you can feel as rested as possible in your 24/7 job as a mum.

Sure, your tiredness might just pass on its own, but maybe getting active about it will help you to feel less like a 'mombie' and more like that woman in full control of her life.

Of course, if you are currently a chronically sleep-deprived mother, it may be a little difficult to follow some of the tools and strategies I offer in this chapter at the moment. The theoretical benefits of getting an extra 45 minutes of slumber, or a sound (albeit short) night's sleep, may feel like too much of a stretch right now. Let me assure you that this is perfectly OK. The tips I offer in this chapter will be here when you're ready, and when you are, it is important to only make one change over a period of time to understand whether it works for you. Too much too soon, and you may cause yourself unnecessary stress, worry, and exhaustion, which defeats the purpose of this chapter altogether.

Coping With Tiredness

Here are my 4 key tips for coping with those days where the walls of your tired bubble seem to get thicker and thicker:

1. Get Active

Moving more can actually help! When you are tired and just lying down or sitting around, it can add to your tiredness. So get out for a short walk with the dog, go for a casual swim, have a session in the garden; even put some fun music on and dance around the house whilst cleaning. I personally find just putting on my runners can motivate me enough to go for a walk on my slower days.

Any of these light activities can lift your energy levels and help you push through the exhaustion.

2. Check your Vitamin and Mineral Levels

As I mentioned, there are many reasons why you might be feeling tired, but making sure that your engines are topped up can be helpful. Whether you are simply dehydrated or are deficient in iron, zinc or some other random thing that your body really needs, you're going to be running on empty.

Drink plenty of water throughout the day and try to see a reputable doctor or naturopath to help you to regain happy body chemistry.

3. Invest in Self-Care

At no other time is it more important to invest in you than when you are depleted of energy and utterly burnt out. Making time to do something low-key that replenishes your 'cup' will get you through the motions of the day by improving your mood, giving you a small burst of energy and allowing you to cope with any motherhood challenges that may come.

Revisit Chapters 4 and 5 if you need tips and strategies to make this happen when you need it the most.

4. Seize Opportunities for Catch Up

Creating or taking advantage of opportunities can help you to catch up on sleep and rest, and get you through the next day or two.

For working mums, taking a personal day (or half-day) for yourself, instead of just for your kids, will give you the time to nap, return chaos to order in your life and regain the energy needed to be more productive back at work and happier at home. I have personally done this a few times since having my kids.

For stay-at-home mums, don't feel guilty or ashamed for asking for help or taking it from those who have already offered. If someone you know and trust can look after the kids for just a few hours, this may be exactly what you need to boost your energy levels and return to a sense of 'normal'. Alternatively, if your kids are still young enough to nap themselves, follow the advice you got in the maternity ward and nap when your baby naps.

Getting Better Sleep

According to Drs. John and Judy Hinwood from the Stress Management Institute, the following quick and easy rituals have been proven to assist in getting to sleep, and encourage better quality sleep:

- Avoid using electronic media for at least an hour or more before bedtime.
- Create your own bedtime routine, which could include deep breathing, reading a few pages from a peaceful or inspiring book, or a calm meditation.
- Wear an eye mask to block out the light.
- Finish your work at least one hour before bed to give your mind a chance to unwind.
- Take a hot bath or shower before bed. The drop in temperature from getting out of the bath signals to your body that it's time for bed.
- Listen to relaxing music.

In addition to these rituals, I have also found that being prepared for a rocky night ahead can help you plan your sleep better. Never gamble on your kids sleeping soundly throughout the night; the odds are likely to be against you. I find that if I expect to be woken or disturbed throughout the night, I am able to plan for it by going to bed early, and I'm more likely to *stick* to that plan. That way, if I'm not woken on a given night, I got bonus sleep — yay! And if I am woken, at least I was prepared for it.

Gratitude, Kindness, and Sleep

So far in this chapter, I have shared with you some highly practical, straight-forward strategies that assist with tiredness and sleep. But they are not the only tips I have to offer.

As it turns out, there is a lot of new research coming out of the field of positive psychology that directly links gratitude and kindness with better sleep outcomes. And it all comes down to the natural chemicals and hormones released into our bodies as a result of these practices. But before I get into the details of how they connect to sleep, let me first share how you can increase your daily expressions of gratitude and kindness.

Gratitude Practice

Having manners and saying 'thank you' was probably ingrained in you as a child. It's the polite and courteous thing to do, right? But how often do you really feel grateful, deep in your heart, and express it?

Funnily enough, not everyone finds it easy to express gratitude. This is largely due to the complex society we live in, with imposed expectations and emotions such as embarrassment, fear-driven obligation, and guilt, which remove the simplicity that expressing gratitude should have. As a result, it can be difficult to develop grateful behaviours naturally.

There are, however, many ways to cultivate gratitude; it's just about finding what is right for you. Some examples include:

- keeping a gratitude journal
- actively noticing or catching things you are grateful for more immediately
- having a gratitude buddy to share your thankfulness with
- counting your blessings during negative times
- being thankful for the lesson a negative situation may have brought you
- literally thanking people more
- writing gratitude letters (and perhaps sending them too!)
- giving gratitude gifts
- giving back to society through volunteering or donating

It's certainly worth investing in your gratitude habits because, as I mentioned, regularly experiencing and expressing gratitude actually contributes to improved sleep quality.

Studies show that when grateful thoughts are brought to mind right before you go to bed, this can lead to better sleep patterns, which are often disturbed when going to bed whilst your brain is still mulling over a problem or issue from the day. When your last thoughts are those of gratitude and appreciation, your thoughts and memories are positive, the part of your brain that regulates emotions and processes stress relief is activated, and your mind becomes calmer, therefore enabling you to enter into a deeper sleep.

> **Meet Claire**
> Claire is a mum of two children in primary school.
> Whilst it has been a few years since Claire's children have woken her up during the night, Claire still finds she sleeps lightly through the night; like her body is on 'alert' in case her kids do wake. Claire also has trouble just 'switching off' her thoughts at night, and will often toss and turn.
> In an effort to increase the quality of her sleep, Claire started compiling a daily gratitude list before bed in a journal. After just one week, Claire found that her mind already felt calmer at bedtime, and she was finally able to reach deeper sleep.

Acts of Kindness

Giving back to society is also a way of practicing kindness, which goes hand in hand with gratitude.

How does performing an act of kindness towards someone make you feel?

People naturally feel good when they give, help or serve others because they experience something called 'helper's high'; a feeling of exhilaration and burst of energy similar to the endorphin-based euphoria experienced after intense exercise, followed by a period of calmness and serenity. This experience is based on an increase of serotonin in your brain, which is a naturally occurring neurochemical that affects, amongst other things, your ability to sleep well.

What's even more amazing is that recent research has also found that people who *observe* an act of kindness also experience similar increases in the production of serotonin!

In addition to the positive effects that kindness practice has on sleep, there is also an abundance of proof that acts of kindness can increase your sense of self-worth, happiness and optimism, and decrease symptoms of depression.

So, here are a few simple suggestions on how to extend the act of kindness to others:

- Smile at strangers; especially those who look like they are having a bad day
- Give compliments often
- Give up your place in line to another person
- Pay for a stranger's coffee
- Donate blood
- Give your seat up for someone on a crowded train or bus
- Pick up 5 pieces of rubbish next time you're out on a walk

- Invite a lonely friend, neighbour or family member over for dinner

And always keep your eyes peeled to observe another's random act of kindness to spur on more acts of good in yourself.

Sleep is a fascinating subject. We all love to sleep and we all want to sleep. And we want our kids to sleep. But this chapter is about you; the tired mum. How you can get better sleep and feel more rested.

I hope that sharing my own experiences with fighting the motherhood sleep deprivation battle, as well as my research into inducing good quality sleep, can start you off on your own journey for getting better sleep than you have had since becoming a mum, and stop you feeling like such a tired mum.

Some of these tips are easy, while others may take a little adjustment and practice, but obviously, a well-rested mum makes for a happier woman, both at home and at work, and a better version of you for your children.

Three actions you can now take:

1. Prepare for a rough night's sleep and plan to get to bed earlier. Reflect on anything that stopped you from doing this and adjust your plan for the following night to try again to make it happen.

2. Write down three things you are grateful for at the end of the day, right before bed, and repeat this every day for the next week.

3. Choose an act of kindness that you are comfortable to perform in the next week, then reflect on how it made you feel.

11

Nurture Your Senses

Throughout the course of motherhood, there are a variety of reasons why you might feel disconnected from your world. The most notable is in the early stages of your journey, where some mothers can feel like they are in 'baby jail'; unable to live outside the 24/7 duties of meeting the fundamental needs of their young infants.

But beyond this time, you can also feel detached well into maternity leave, when you're at home looking after your children when they are sick, when family members and friends are away for extended periods of time or when your partner is away at work more often than usual.

Lack of connection from the people that are normally around you is probably the most noticeable cause of feeling lost or alone as a mum, but there are less obvious detachments that occur that can also contribute to feeling this way; detachments from things and experiences that help remind you of who you are, what you love, the emotions you are experiencing and your very worthy existence in this world.

Meet Rebecca
Rebecca is a working mum of one, with a bub on the way.

Rebecca's days are full of work and home duties, spending time with her partner and looking after/playing with her son.

Although she is happy with her work-life balance, enjoys her job and loves spending quality time with her little boy, Rebecca still feels detached from her sense of self.

Whilst she does occasionally get some 'me' time, Rebecca always feels like she is catching up with life during this time, rather than truly nourishing her soul.

Rebecca is searching for ways to reconnect with herself and her world.

In the first chapter of this book I pointed out that after we become mums, we often don't give ourselves the time to rediscover who we are, now that we are parents. In the ongoing chaos of motherhood, you can also forget to regularly reconnect with the things that nourish and ground you as an individual human being; the things in life that can make you feel fully alive and awake.

♥ ♥ ♥

If you are like most mums today, you probably believe your kids are the most important people in your family. It's true that they are usually the loudest and most demanding, but the most important? You love your kids so much that you want to make them happy and give them everything, but to put them first all of the time is detrimental to your own mental health, happiness and life satisfaction.

You and your family do not exist because of your kids; your kids actually exist because of *you*, and they will thrive because of the stable family you have built. Your kids wouldn't eat well, have nice clothing to wear, live in a nice home, and enjoy vacations without *you*. The most important person in an army is the General. The most important person in a corporation is the CEO. The most important person in a classroom is the teacher. And the most important people in a family are the parents.

By sacrificing everything for your children, you are also giving up two of the most valuable connections to the things that make you, you. Simple things in life that can remind you of who you are, boost your mood, ground you in reality and make you see and appreciate the amazing parts to your existence. Music, and the natural world.

Humans have always had a special relationship with music, in some form or another. Music plays a big part in life, and is so ingrained in everyday life that it's almost hard to imagine an activity that is not accompanied by it; it can be heard while you shop, study, work, travel, socialise, relax or exercise. This is because studies in psychology, neuroscience, and medicine all acknowledge the power of music to significantly enhance our state of body and mind.

Although you spend most of your time surrounded by music, being fully engaged in your own personal choice in music can deeply connect with who you are. It's through this increased level of engagement with music that the disconnection from your world dissipates, and can also boost your mood, improve your exercise outcomes, motivate you and heal your psyche.

But when was the last time you consciously made the choice to play a song or piece of music that *you* love to listen to? Life as a mum doesn't have to always be about nursery rhymes and Wiggles songs. And whilst I can relate to your desire to embrace silence in the small moments you manage to find it, playing music that you love to listen, sing or dance to may just be the remedy to stress, a flat mood or feelings of disconnection that you are truly in need of.

In the first part of this chapter, I'm not only going to outline *why* music is so important for your health and happiness as a mum; I'll also go through the different ways you can create opportunities to regularly reconnect with the music *you* love to feel more alive and connected with who you are.

As a mum, you often hear the endless pleas from child psychologists, and other childhood development professionals, to ensure our kids are given plenty of opportunities to play and explore the outdoors, but did you know how beneficial experiencing nature can be for *you*?

In Chapter 4, I discussed the prevalence of loneliness and isolation in motherhood. In addition to losses of friendships and reduced contact with other adults, mums can also feel alone in their world as a result of not being *in* it.

Connecting with nature can be extremely beneficial for your body, your brain, your overall wellness, and life satisfaction. Sadly, mums tend to underestimate the amazing benefits of having brief and regular contact with nature for themselves, and not just for their kids.

The second part of this chapter will show you exactly *how* interacting with your natural environment can ground and reinvigorate your sense of wellbeing. I'll also walk you through some of the easiest ways you can connect with nature more regularly in your busy life as a mum so that you can feel more relaxed, self-aware and connected with the world around you.

Reconnect With Music

Do you love to dance? To sing? To tap your foot or bop your head to a strong, steady beat?

I love to do all three! And I can almost guarantee you that most people will say yes to at least one of these questions. This is because music is a powerful communication system that directly speaks to the parts of your brain that process emotion.

Music affects us in such a profound way because it stimulates your body's natural feel-good chemicals (endorphins and oxytocin), which can alter your mood, provide an outlet for you to take control of your feelings and even help you to work through problems. The effectiveness of music, however, is largely dictated by you having a choice in what is played.

Listening to music is a popular way to cope with difficult times; perhaps to express how you are feeling or to vent difficult thoughts and emotions. Certain pieces of music can affect you in deeply personal ways; it might be tied to a memory of someone or moment in time, or perhaps you feel the lyrics of a song are speaking directly to you and find comfort within them. I personally find that belting out lyrics at the top of my lungs, rather than just listening to a song, can be very therapeutic during times of high stress, frustration or overwhelming joy. The release of such strong emotions is very liberating for me and gives me a healthy mechanism through which I can process and express these emotions.

When you feel down, it can be tempting to play music that fits with how you feel, or that relates to a time when you have felt like this in the past, which may make you feel worse. Some music may allow you to sit with a mood, explore it, understand it, and not feel worse from doing so. But it can be much more helpful to choose music that is *not* close to how you feel now and is just slightly above it. For instance, a song that is a little faster or slightly more upbeat, or a piece of music that starts slow and sad, but picks up in tempo throughout, so it can influence your mood in the same way.

Music choices can also relax or energise you. The rhythm of a song can affect your pulse and respiration rates so they are in time with the beat or rhythm, therefore naturally improving your energy levels at times where you might feel slow or tired. Also, if a piece of music increases your mood, so too will it raise your energy levels.

> **Meet Bianca**
> Bianca is a mum of a school-aged child and a toddler.
> During school holidays, Bianca gets very tired, stressed and down looking after both of her kids 24/7.
> As a quick and easy pick-me-up, Bianca puts on one of her favourite CDs each day. Occasionally she sings the lyrics to her kids, and even gets them up dancing with her around the lounge room!
> Music helps Bianca get through each day as something to look forward to, and a way of connecting with both herself and her kids.

Just in case I haven't convinced you yet to start putting yourself above the kids for a change when it comes to playing music, here is another fantastic reason; across the world, music therapy and music medicine strategies have found that choosing the right music can improve your sleep quality. So in addition to the strategies I provided in the previous chapter to help you get better sleep, music can help with this too!

As you can see, making time in your hectic life as a mum to play your favourite music can be one of the most effective and enjoyable ways to improve your happiness and health. However it is important to understand that to really unlock the benefits that music can bring, you need to actively listen to it and give it your full attention, rather than simply using it as background noise.

Since becoming a mum, and even more so since my second child, I have found that I play *my* music less and less often. Life becomes very 'noisy' with conversations, arguments, TV, phone calls — and then there's the need for silence at times. But I have also found that consciously deciding to hit play on a favourite CD in my car, or pop my earbuds in and divert all calls on my phone for a short time during the day is well worth the effort. I feel happier and more relaxed, but more importantly, I feel like *me* again.

Music is very personal to each of us, and what affects one person in one way, may affect someone else very differently. You probably have some idea of what affects you and how, but you can experiment and try out different pieces of music.

Try creating different playlists on your phone, iPad or computer according to your different moods:
- lighter and faster music for when you're feeling sad
- calming music for when you're feeling tense, or having trouble falling asleep
- vibrant music to wake you up
- happy music with a good beat to energise you, or make you feel like dancing
- loud, strong music to vent frustration or stress

Keep these playlists handy so you can easily start playing them any time you need them, anywhere you are, such as at home, in bed, driving the car, waiting in the school carpark, going for a walk or playing with your children.

Reconnect With Nature

Studies have shown that if you look at an image of a natural environment, as opposed to an image of an urban concrete street, your stress levels drop and your mood and energy levels improve because you are allowing your brain to dial down and rest, like an overused muscle.

Rachel and Stephen Kaplan, professors of psychology at the University of Michigan and specialists in environmental psychology, explain that your brain understands that natural environments contain highly complex sensory inputs and innately refuses to interpret or make sense of them, so it relaxes. And that's just by *looking* at nature!

But before you go changing the home screens on your computer, iPad, and phone, browsing nature photographs or watching a nature documentary to improve your mood and de-stress (which are still great ideas!), actually getting outdoors and connecting directly with natural environments will provide you with much greater benefits.

When was the last time you spent some quality time immersed in nature? How regularly do you do this?

After just 20 minutes of spending time in nature, you'll probably notice:

- reduced tension in your muscles
- reduced heart rate (and subsequently, decreased blood pressure)
- improvements in your concentration
- positive emotions and mood
- increased levels of happiness
- decreased feelings of anxiety, and
- improvements in your memory function

I'm sure I don't need to tell you how amazing these benefits are to a busy mum like you! So let's get to how you can make sure you're reconnecting with the world around you on a daily basis. It's actually very simple; here are some low-cost, low-effort ideas to get you started:

- just go and sit within a natural surrounding
- go for a walk/run/bike ride to move your body within nature
- wiggle your toes in the grass
- sink your fingers into rich, crumbly soil in the garden
- watch sea foam wash over your feet as you stroll along a beach

- get outside on your lunch-break
- go for a picnic
- swim in a natural body of water (lake/river/ocean)
- do some gardening
- pick and smell flowers
- go fruit picking at a local orchid/farm
- go stargazing on a clear night

The possibilities and opportunities are endless! In this beautiful country, most of you would have access to some form of urban park, community garden, conservation area, or backyard. Nature experiences in these spaces offer opportunities to take many parts of your daily routine from indoors to outdoors quite easily.

But what if the weather is bad outside? Try these ideas to get your nature-fix:

- put on some gumboots and splash about in the puddles
- open a window and let some fresh air into your home
- nurture an indoor garden; windowsill herbs or hardy succulents are great options
- sit by a window with garden views
- get up and watch the sunrise, or pause to watch the sunset

It is part of my day now that I get outdoors at least once. I get so much joy, renewed energy, calm and clarity from briefly pausing at some point during my day to go outside and pay attention to the colours, smells and sounds around me. I love feeling the sun or the rain on my skin or letting my thoughts just wander for a few moments to casually observe what's going on in the world, outside of my mind. I find these experiences very grounding and helpful in managing overwhelm from my mummy mental load, regain focus when I'm trying to make a decision or to simply feel connected with the world again, and my existence within it.

♥ ♥ ♥

There is a tremendous amount of power in music. From the stories told through lyrics, or atmospheres generated by concerts, to feeling rhythms and beats inside your body, and personally creating sounds, music can help to re-establish and strengthen the connection with your true self and to feel like you again.

The same amount of power can be found in your relationship with nature. As humans, we have an innate desire to connect and seek out natural surroundings, but the chaos of life as a mother can suck away the little windows of time that you might otherwise use to be outside. Nurturing your nature relationship will not only promote relaxation and restoration, but bring awareness to your 'aliveness' and connection to the complex, yet wondrous, environment within which you live.

♥ ♥ ♥

Three actions you can now take:

1. Dig out an old CD or album on your computer, iPad or phone and play it every time you drive somewhere for a few days.

2. Have a go at creating one or two playlists for different emotions or situations.

3. Choose one daily activity that you would normally do indoors and start regularly taking it outside.

12

Eat With Your Mind

I'm sure you've seen many celebrities give birth and then somehow seem to have a super-human ability to return to their pre-pregnancy size and shape within weeks. Women from many South East Asian cultures also seem to have this ability. But for the everyday mum, this ability to regain our pre-pregnancy figure is often unachievable, leaving you to feel unhappy and disheartened.

Your desire to lose weight is not just about the aesthetic appeal of looking like you did before you became a mum; it's also about trying to regain a sense of who you are. You look in the mirror and no longer recognise yourself. Inside, you can feel like you've lost your spark, your 'pep', your uniqueness — and returning to a physical familiarity seems like a logical place to look for them.

Although almost two-thirds of new mums wish to return to their pre-pregnancy size and shape just weeks after giving birth, I wasn't one of them. I was a long-term breastfeeder, so it wasn't until a few weeks after each of my breastfeeding journeys that I felt the desire to do something about my body. For me, it was more than wanting to look good and feel like me again; I just wanted to be fit enough to keep up with my kids, have the capacity to do anything in life with them and be a good role model for them in the process.

Like many new mums, you probably tried to go on a diet soon after having your children to return to your previous body shape. And for most mums, the diet didn't work and actually made our relationship with food a whole lot worse than it ever was.

Do you frequently eat off your child's plate? Hate to see good food go to waste, or simply don't find the time to eat a proper meal yourself?

I can relate. Fussy children, the effort I have put into cooking a good meal for them and a day where time has not been on my side leads to this habit regularly. Then, when I do get the time to eat something, I'm so tired that I don't really feel like preparing something healthy and nutritious to eat, and the easiest things to grab tend to be the exact opposite;

fast, cheap and unhealthy. And then I accidentally eat too much of it.

♥ ♥ ♥

Let me first explain that these celebrities and South East Asian women aren't super-human. They just have access to one, so to speak. Celebrities use expensive fitness coaches, and in South East Asian countries it is a common tradition for someone called a 'confinement lady' to move into the family home for a month immediately after the birth of a child to manage a mother and her baby. Her work includes getting a woman's physique back into shape. After that, the woman and her baby are ready to meet the world.

But most Australian mums don't have these luxuries. We often return home within days of giving birth with minimal support and guidance from health professionals, who focus primarily on healthy weight gain and feeding of your baby, look out for red flags in terms of your mental health and educate you in handling any post-partum physical issues.

Regardless of whether your body shape desires start immediately after pregnancy or years later, and what is fuelling these desires, it is fundamentally important to understand that a mother's weight gain or obesity does *not* stem from pregnancy itself. According to a study in 2017 by

Dr. Olga Yakusheva, associate professor at the University of Michigan's School of Nursing, mums gain weight in the first few years after childbirth as a result of lifestyle choices related to putting the needs of their children first, and subsequently not exercising or taking care of themselves.

With this understanding, you can start to see why eating food off your child's plate and responding to cravings during times of sleep deprivation work against you in your battle with weight gain and body image. To add to this, age is strongly correlated with weight changes, so the more time you have spent in motherhood, the harder it becomes to lose and maintain weight effectively.

Despite your best attempts to be fit and healthy after kids, do you always seem to end up back where you started, or more frustratingly, further behind?

Your mind is the most powerful tool you have in living healthy. It is more powerful than exercise, food and any other thing you may have tried. Why? Because your mind controls everything you do; let me explain this further.

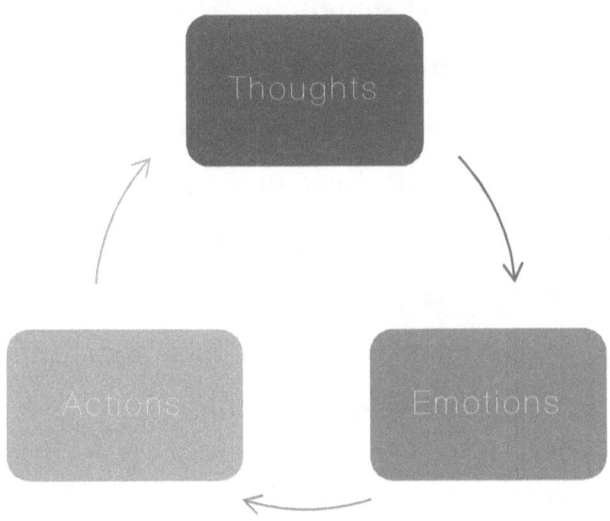

Your mind controls what you are unconsciously and consciously thinking. These thoughts spark emotions inside of you, which then drive your actions. Your actions and behaviours then reinforce your initial thoughts, as well as new ones.

So your mind strongly influences the choices you make, and can actually play against you when trying to actively change behaviours, such as eating healthy and exercise habits for weight loss and fitness.

In this final chapter, I will go through the most common ways your mind can sabotage your efforts in losing weight, getting fit and eating healthier. I'll also provide you with practical ways to overcome these acts of sabotage to achieve your goals in this area.

I acknowledge that sometimes, after having children, it's not so much that you *can't* lose the weight, but you now have less time to go to the gym or a fitness class, less time to food shop properly, and less time to prepare healthy meals. If finding time to do these things is far more crucial to your success in having a healthy body than mind-based sabotage, I encourage you to refer back to the tools, tips, and strategies provided in Chapter Five in this book.

♥ ♥ ♥

I need to start off by saying that there is *nothing wrong with the way you look*.

Your post-partum body has stretched, transformed, grown and supported new life. It might rock stretch marks or scars, and be extremely tired at times, but your body is superhero-strong, beautiful and something to be extremely proud of. You carried and birthed a child (if not more than one); new curves and abilities should be expected!

It's completely normal to occasionally think about how your body looked before, but your children should be a reminder of just how much your body is capable of, and how it will continue to evolve.

Ways Your Mind Can Sabotage You

Read through the following five mind patterns, and if one or more of them feel very familiar to you, the next section will provide you with helpful ways to change the way your mind is operating in order to change your lifestyle behaviours to be more positive.

1. Self-Dislike

You can't get your dislike for your body off your mind. Every time you think about your body, you feel cranky, sad, rejected, hopeless and fearful. You may not be voicing your self-dislike for your body to your friends or your partner, but internally you are being the nastiest friend that you know to yourself.

As you eat meals, wash in the shower, moisturise, get dressed and exercise, the nasty thoughts circulate. It's the last thing that you feel when you go to sleep, and it doesn't feel good. It makes you unhappy and hurt.

2. Self-Doubt

After past attempts at losing weight and living healthy, you are starting to doubt your ability to be successful; or if you even deserve to be. You might push on, thinking "this (insert your new thing) will work", however, your self-doubt is usually still unconsciously present. You start to judge others who seem to have it all, giving yourself very good reasons why it works for them, why it's ok for them and why their 'situation' is the reason it works for them. But you are just feeding your self-doubt further.

Eventually, your self-doubt can be overwhelming and you feel like the gap is just too big. So you either stop, or you try another 'new thing' to have a healthy body. And the cycle goes on....

3. Negative Self-Talk

Feel like your mind is much like the movie 'Inside Out'?
That voice inside your head always seems to have something negative to say. You often hear words like 'can't', 'sorry', 'should', 'must', 'hope' and 'maybe'. You seem to concentrate a lot on your mistakes, and immediately interpret criticisms and comments negatively.

You tend to see all the bad things that happen to you as permanent, and frequently generalise them to other aspects of your life, for example, "I screwed up again; I always screw up; I'm not good at anything." You also see the good things in your life as temporary, for example, "Exercising is fun, for now; I'll probably get over it soon."

4. Misdirected Beliefs

Making excuses has become easy. The more you do it, the more believable they have become. Sayings like "I can't lose weight", "Exercise is boring", "I don't like fruit and vegetables",

"I'm too tired", "I have no time", "It's selfish", "What's the point, I know I'll fail" are common. They feel real to your mind and are very familiar.

In addition to excuses, you also lie to yourself on a regular basis to justify your actions. You feed yourself lies so you can feed yourself unhealthy habits, somewhat guilt-free. You tell yourself things like "I've eaten so good today, I can afford it", "At least they are healthy snacks", "It's probably not that many calories", "I'll just have a few" and "I can run it off in the morning."

I am notoriously bad when it comes to making excuses and lying to myself when it comes to eating healthy and exercising. Having lost 16kgs before having my son, and reaching a fitness level that allowed me to go to 1-hour group fitness classes five times a week, I know how good it can feel to reach this standard of living. But getting the momentum going again, after finishing my breastfeeding journey with my son, has been riddled with excuses and lies. I know I'm doing it, but once I start, it's hard to break the habit.

5. Weight Focused

You focus a lot on weight loss and numbers, and your best and worst actions fluctuate with your weight. When you are feeling bad about your weight and body, you begin a health kick. When you begin to feel ok, you stop your health kick and you end up where you were. Or, when you're feeling ok and eating well, but your emotions flat line or normalise (as they do from time to time), your worst actions prevail and you 'fall off the wagon'.

How to Control the Power Of Your Mind

Now that you understand a little bit about how your mind is working against you and your desires to eat and live healthily, let's take a look at ways you can redirect the control your mind has over your actions and outcomes.

Start With Energy

Without energy, you will give in to your negative mind patterns and bad habits every time. Nourish your body with whole foods, enough sleep, stress relief strategies, hydration and regular exercise when your body needs it. Invest in taking care of yourself emotionally, physically, mentally and spiritually.

When I am feeling low in energy, sleep-deprived, stressed out, bloated from overeating high-fat foods or crashing from too much sugar I definitely lack the motivation to do anything positive for myself. Even as someone with relatively high self-esteem, my self-confidence can take a huge hit and self-doubt can kick in. Getting on top of my energy leaks is paramount for me to be able to create motivation and momentum toward my healthy living goals.

Previous chapters in this book can help with these forms of self-nourishment; in particular, Chapter Nine.

Celebrate Progress

For many mums, having kids brings the cessation of employment and some friendships, and for a long part of your life, you have gained your self-worth from other people's words, acknowledgments and appreciation. When that ceases, who are you? What is your worth?

Women, and mums in particular, are very energised by achievement. But the self-worth you are seeking actually comes from what *you* think and tell yourself. Be kind and focus on what you are achieving. If no one else is telling you 'well-done', be sure to tell yourself in some way; treat yourself to coffee and cake, a movie, a long, hot shower or a glass of wine. Celebrate your successes in a deliberate and open way. This will not only build self-worth but also your self-esteem and self-confidence.

Practice using Kind Words

Self-talk is actually one of the most effective forms of cognitive coping with setbacks in life, as long as it's positive, with words like 'want', 'can' and 'will'. When your voice inside your head is talking positively, it is considering bad things as temporary and seeing them as isolated. For example, "The weather caused it", "That was a rough couple of hours", and "That wasn't so great, but I can do better next time." It is also considering good things to be permanent changes, for example, "I've done well with this; now I know how to do it."

Some strategies to counteract or change the negative messages being sent by your mind to be more positive include:

- reminding yourself of past, related events where you were successful in achieving something
- reminding yourself of all the skills you have to perform well with
- quickly interrupting thoughts with a verbal phrase like "I Reject It", or a tactile reaction like flicking a rubber band on your wrist, then replacing the thought with something positive
- daily practice of positive affirmations, such as "I am a strong, beautiful woman and a great mum" or "I am doing a great job"

Thought Flipping

When you start to hear any of the regular excuses you give yourself for not eating healthy or exercising, force your mind to replace the thought with its healthier version. For example:

- "I can't lose weight" > "I can lose weight whenever I want"
- "Exercise is boring" > "There are types of exercise that I enjoy"
- "I hate fruit and vegetables" > "Vegetables and fruit keep me healthy"
- "What's the point, I know I'll fail" > "I can achieve whatever I put my mind to"

And if you catch yourself in an internal lie, try telling yourself the truth:

- "I've eaten so well today, I can afford it" > "I've eaten so well today, I will protect my hard work"
- "At least they are healthy snacks" > "I can get fat on healthy foods too"
- "It's probably not that many calories" > "It's probably a lot more calories than I think"
- "I'll just have a few" > "I never have just a few; I will end up having 'just a little more'"
- "I can run it off in the morning" > "I should run off what I've already eaten"

Focus On Health

If your intention behind every action becomes health (rather than weight), your actions become consistent. When you link your actions to weight, rather than 'health', you will always ride the rollercoaster of reacting to the highs and lows in life with your eating and exercise habits.

You attract what you think about. Whether it is the thought of wanting 'not' to be overweight, or thinking and worrying about being overweight, you are attracting 'weight'. Focus on wanting to be healthy and fit, and your perceptions and goals will change as well.

This shift in focus was the key to my success in creating a healthy lifestyle prior to having my son. Having a goal to look, feel and be fit was far more important to me as a mum of one, preparing to fall pregnant again with my second. I wanted to have as much energy as possible to continue doing fun things with my daughter throughout my pregnancy; I even made it to my third trimester still participating in Zumba classes!

Food Recall

Appetite is formed in the mind as much as it is in the stomach. You retain sensory memory of the food you have eaten, therefore you can control the majority of your hunger pains if you focus on remembering the sensations felt when you last ate.

This process is similar to meditation and, as a result, you will feel less of a need to consume more. Keeping a food journal can also be helpful with this.

Create Behaviours That Change Your Mind

So now you have insight into how your mind is sabotaging your efforts to live healthier and ways to gain back control over your mind and its emotion-generating thoughts, which are influencing any actions you take. Lastly, if you refer back to the cycle illustrated at the start of this chapter, you will also see that your actions and behaviours can either reinforce your initial thoughts or influence new ones.

Here are 10 easily actionable changes to make to your routine that can assist in generating helpful thoughts and create a positive cycle for healthy living habits:

1. Eat more filling meals, particularly at dinner time
2. Keep it out of your house; you wouldn't stock up on alcohol if you were a recovering alcoholic, so don't stock up on snacks if you are a recovering foodie (this is a huge one for me)

3. Change your food choices; trade high-calorie foods for healthier options

4. Stick to pre-packaged foods if you have a problem with stopping

5. Avoid alcohol; the relaxation you feel from a glass of wine is just enough to make you 'relaxed' about your eating habits

6. Start new habits when you would normally reach for food; do productive things that keep you busy, like stretching while watching TV, doing a mani/pedi, fold clothes, sip on hot tea, etc.

7. Reduce TV time; if you struggle with eating while watching TV, take a long relaxing bath, spend some quiet time with your partner, or play a board game with your kids, walk the dog or do a yoga routine on YouTube

8. Go to bed; you burn more calories sleeping than sitting on the couch and feeling rested means you have more resilience to face the next day with

9. Get the support you need; talk with the people you live with and let them know the changes you are making so they can support (or join) you in your goal to live healthier

10. Play slow music during meal times; you are naturally encouraged to eat slower and give your body a chance to detect when you are full to avoid overeating

McDonald's did their own research, which showed that we eat according to the speed of the music being played. Therefore, when a restaurant is busy with a queue building up, McDonald's plays fast music, thus ensuring that the customers will eat quickly, and leave the restaurant sooner, freeing up the table for the next customers.

♥ ♥ ♥

I am currently on my next big healthy living journey, since finishing up breastfeeding my son last year. Reflecting on my underlying thoughts and subsequent behaviours is important to understand what I need to do to break bad habits and create new positive ones.

Healthy eating and exercise habits require a commitment to constant work-in-progress. Over time, habits become more ingrained and need less effort to maintain, but life's ups and downs can throw you out of balance at any point; particularly as a mum already juggling so much on your plate.

Your mind is a powerful machine, capable of influencing each emotion you feel and action you take in life. But reconfiguring the machine is not impossible; knowing how to do it and practicing regularly is the key to achieving your own healthy living goals.

♥ ♥ ♥

Three actions you can now take:

1. Assess your own levels of energy and stress using the previous chapters in this book to determine how ready you are to make healthy lifestyle changes.

2. Create a list of phrases or activities you will use to congratulate yourself with for any achievements you have each day and start using them.

3. Choose one actionable change you would like to make to your routine from the list provided and practice this change for the next 30 days to create a positive habit.

Afterword

How awesome are you, Mum! You have made it to the end of this life-changing book. Congratulations! I am truly proud that you are taking steps towards being a happier, balanced woman with children. And you should certainly be proud too!

This book had distinct themes in it. You read about becoming clear on who you are outside of being a mum, handling your mental load and stress, living mindfully, investing in self-care and 'me' time, controlling emotions such as guilt and frustration, strengthening relationships, loving what you do, finding more energy, getting better quality sleep, staying connected with your world and your soul, and harnessing the power of your mind.

All of these concepts are important — but was there something else you noticed?

Having a happy, balanced life as a mum takes commitment, and new habits take a little time to form. Be kind to yourself, start with small changes and build from there. I achieved balance in small areas of my life before I started living in overall equilibrium. And at times, something new will come along in my life to shift my balance and control.

I want you to know that the strategies in this book *do* work and will continue to do so as long as you keep them up.

I admire women that give something a good go; that commit and stick out the early days of making a change. There is something to learn in every experience and in every stage of motherhood. Take those learnings, adjust, pick yourself up, and do it again.

Your perceived shortcomings, failures and setbacks are just that; *perceived*. But they will make you a wiser mother, partner, work colleague, friend, and ultimately provide you with the best personal development journey you have ever had. If, after a little while, something isn't working, try something else. If it *is* working, keep it up! It's as simple as that.

I'd love to hear how you have gone with what I have been teaching you, so make sure you drop me a quick message via social media or my contact details in this book. What was your favourite strategy? Have you used one and amended it for yourself that is working wonders now? Tell me about it; I am always on a learning curve myself and looking for fresh, new ideas on how to keep living a happy, fulfilling, balanced life as a mum.

I look forward to hearing about your journey soon.

Love Nikki xxx

I'd love to hear your feedback about what worked in your life. Please post your wins on my Facebook page at
www.facebook.com/morethanamumwellness/
or send me an email to
morethanamum@nikkicox.com.au

About The Author

Nikki Cox was born in Melbourne, Victoria and raised throughout coastal and country Victoria with her three younger siblings. At the age of twenty-three, Nikki met her now-husband whilst online gaming and took the leap of faith to move to sunny Queensland to start a new phase in her life.

At thirty, Nikki fell pregnant and had her first child, and, for the first time since moving interstate, found it challenging to be so far away from her family during these important milestones in her life.

Through her own struggles with becoming a mum, and losing a sense of her identity and self-worth, Nikki found that there was very little support for mothers beyond the first 2 years. Nikki made it her mission to find the help she needed, and now empowers other women on their journey through motherhood in their own wellness in order to live happier, healthier and in balance.

Nikki is inspirational and engaging, and has such a powerful and positive impact on mothers. Working with Nikki will give you the opportunity to talk about yourself and your life in a comfortable, friendly and safe space, in ways you never have before.

For many years, Nikki has been teaching practical identity discovery, self-care and emotional balance techniques that really work. They will lead you out of the stress and confusion around being a mum and into a balanced life using simple and sustainable tools and strategies. You will be amazed how easy and practical the techniques are, and how you can apply them in your busy mum life.

Nikki has spent over 10 years in adult learning and development, has higher education degrees in psychology and wellness, and is a qualified wellness coach with the International Coaching Federation. Her experience as an education professional, a mother of two, a sufferer of Fibromyalgia for over 15 years, and an inspirational coach has given her an awesome array of tools for her own success through motherhood, as well as for many others.

Learn from this very talented and highly experienced Wellness Lifestyle educator, coach and author how to rediscover the woman within and make simple lifestyle changes as a busy mum for greater happiness, energy and control over life.

You can connect with me at:

www.morethanamum.com.au

www.facebook.com/morethanamumwellness/

www.instagram.com/morethanamumwellness/

Work With Nikki

More Than A Mum workshops

    Low in energy?

    Lacking in time?

    Feeling passionless?

    Want more control in life?

    Looking for something for YOU?

More Than A Mum workshops will empower you further to make positive changes in your life using practical, real-world tips, tools and strategies, which are easy to do, even as a busy Mum. You will connect with like-minded mums and learn how to:

- find more energy and zest for life
- let go of unnecessary stress
- overcome feelings of guilt and selfishness

…and so much more.

Strictly limited places available. For more information, visit www.morethanamum.com.au/workshops

Personal Coaching

For you to be able to focus on yourself and create new goals, paths and habits, you may need the help of a coach.

> As a coach, I *listen*.
> As a coach, I ask *powerful, intuitive questions*.
> As a coach, I *support, challenge, and motivate* you to make positive changes in your life.
> As a coach, I provide *a succinct, efficient service*, because I understand time is in short supply as a mother and support is needed in real-time.

Wellness lifestyle coaching can be an incredibly powerful experience for a busy mum. How often can you create space in your life to regularly talk about all the things you want, the things that scare you, the things you want to change AND do that with a powerful ally, who wants to see you succeed?

My 1-on-1 coaching sessions run for 30 minutes at a time and are conducted over the phone, so they fit easily into your busy life as a mum. You will be provided with deeper, more personalised support in developing goals to discovering yourself again, and live the life *you* want, beyond being a mum.

To find a coaching package that's right for you, visit www.morethanamum.com.au/coaching

Post-Parental Leave Coaching

Working with a variety of employers, Nikki delivers highly successful coaching programs to provide practical, 1-on-1 support for mothers returning to work following parental leave to assist with mental load management, achieving work-life equilibrium and overcoming feelings of guilt, self-doubt, and self-confidence.

Post-parental leave coaching supports mothers in reducing the stress associated with their return, reignites passion for work, thereby increasing long and short-term employee retention rates, and presenteeism.

If you, or your employer, are interested in finding out more about post-parental leave coaching support for mothers, please email nikki@nikkicox.com.au

Speaking

Looking for a speaker for your next conference, workshop or meeting?

If you would like to give Nikki the mic and have her speak at your next event on any of the topics covered in this book, please email nikki@nikkicox.com.au

Contributions

Nikki has extensive experience as a valued contributor to a wide variety of publications.

If you would like Nikki to submit an article, participate in an interview or provide a quote for your publication, please email nikki@nikkicox.com.au

NIKKI COX

www.ingramcontent.com/pod-product-compliance
Lightning Source LLC
Chambersburg PA
CBHW031415290426
44110CB00011B/395